LET'S celebrate

Name _____

Message _____

_____

_____

Email / Phone _____

Name _____

Message _____

_____

_____

Email / Phone _____

Name _____

Message _____

_____

_____

Email / Phone _____

A birthday is a time to reflect on the year gone by, but to also set your goals for the upcoming year. __Catherine Pulsifer

Name _____

Message _____

_____

_____

Email / Phone _____

Name _____

Message _____

_____

_____

Email / Phone _____

Name _____

Message _____

_____

_____

Email / Phone _____

To know how to grow old is the master-work of wisdom, and one of the most difficult chapters is the great art of living. _Henri Frederic Amiel

Name _____

Message _____

_____

_____

Email / Phone _____

Name _____

Message _____

_____

_____

Email / Phone _____

Name _____

Message _____

_____

_____

Email / Phone _____

As you grow older, may you grow richer in all of the most important things in life.
- Unknown

Name _____

Message _____

_____

_____

Email / Phone _____

Name _____

Message _____

_____

_____

Email / Phone _____

Name _____

Message _____

_____

_____

Email / Phone _____

Your past is not your potential. In any hour you can choose to liberate the future.
- Marilyn Ferguson

Name _____

Message _____

_____

_____

Email / Phone _____

Name _____

Message _____

_____

_____

Email / Phone _____

Name _____

Message _____

_____

_____

Email / Phone _____

To keep the heart unwrinkled, to be hopeful, kindly, cheerful, reverent that is triumph our old age. *–Thomas H. Aldrich*

Name _____

Message _____

_____

_____

Email / Phone _____

Name _____

Message _____

_____

_____

Email / Phone _____

Name _____

Message _____

_____

_____

Email / Phone _____

Aging is not lost youth but a new stage of opportunity and strength.
- Betty Friedan

Name _____

Message _____

_____

_____

Email / Phone _____

Name _____

Message _____

_____

_____

Email / Phone _____

Name _____

Message _____

_____

_____

Email / Phone _____

It takes courage to grow up and be who you really are.
- E.E. Cummings

Name _____

Message _____

_____

_____

Email / Phone _____

Name _____

Message _____

_____

_____

Email / Phone _____

Name _____

Message _____

_____

_____

Email / Phone _____

Your past is not your potential. In any hour you can choose to liberate the future.
- Marilyn Ferguson

Name _____

Message _____

_____

_____

Email / Phone _____

Name _____

Message _____

_____

_____

Email / Phone _____

Name _____

Message _____

_____

_____

Email / Phone _____

God give us the gift of life; it is up to us to give ourselves the gift of living well. -*Voltaire*

Name _____

Message _____

_____

_____

Email / Phone _____

Name _____

Message _____

_____

_____

Email / Phone _____

Name _____

Message _____

_____

_____

Email / Phone _____

The more you praise and celebrate your life, the more there is in life to celebrate.
-Oprah Winfrey

Name _____

Message _____

_____

_____

Email / Phone _____

Name _____

Message _____

_____

_____

Email / Phone _____

Name _____

Message _____

_____

_____

Email / Phone _____

A gift consists not in what is done or given, but is the intention of the giver or doer. *_ Lucius Annaeus Seneca*

Name _____

Message _____

_____

_____

Email / Phone _____

Name _____

Message _____

_____

_____

Email / Phone _____

Name _____

Message _____

_____

_____

Email / Phone _____

Success is like reaching an important birthday and finding you're exactly the same.
_ Audrey Hepburn

Name _____

Message _____

_____

_____

Email / Phone _____

Name _____

Message _____

_____

_____

Email / Phone _____

Name _____

Message _____

_____

_____

Email / Phone _____

Our birthdays are feathers in broad wing of time.
- Jean Paul Richter

Name _____

Message _____

_____

_____

Email / Phone _____

Name _____

Message _____

_____

_____

Email / Phone _____

Name _____

Message _____

_____

_____

Email / Phone _____

Don't just count your years, make your years count.
-Ernest Meyers

Name _____

Message _____

_____

_____

Email / Phone _____

Name _____

Message _____

_____

_____

Email / Phone _____

Name _____

Message _____

_____

_____

Email / Phone _____

Age is strictly a case of mind over matter. If you don't mind, it doesn't matter.
- Jack Benny

Name _____

Message _____

_____

_____

Email / Phone _____

Name _____

Message _____

_____

_____

Email / Phone _____

Name _____

Message _____

_____

_____

Email / Phone _____

> **Whatever with the past has gone, the best is always yet to come.**
> **- Lucy Larcom**

Name _____

Message _____

_____

_____

Email / Phone _____

Name _____

Message _____

_____

_____

Email / Phone _____

Name _____

Message _____

_____

_____

Email / Phone _____

A birthday is a time to reflect on the year gone by, but to also set your goals for the upcoming year. *--Catherine Pulsifer*

Name _____

Message _____

_____

_____

Email / Phone _____

Name _____

Message _____

_____

_____

Email / Phone _____

Name _____

Message _____

_____

_____

Email / Phone _____

You are never too old to set another goal or to dream a new dream.
-Les Brown

Name _____

Message _____

_____

_____

Email / Phone _____

Name _____

Message _____

_____

_____

Email / Phone _____

Name _____

Message _____

_____

_____

Email / Phone _____

When you were born, you cried and the world rejoiced. Live your life so that when you die, the world cries and you rejoice. - *Cherokee Expression*

Name _____

Message _____

_____

_____

Email / Phone _____

Name _____

Message _____

_____

_____

Email / Phone _____

Name _____

Message _____

_____

_____

Email / Phone _____

May you live all the days of your life.
- Jonathan Swift

Name _____

Message _____

_____

_____

Email / Phone _____

Name _____

Message _____

_____

_____

Email / Phone _____

Name _____

Message _____

_____

_____

Email / Phone _____

Everyday is a birthday; every moment of it is new to us; we are born again, renewed for fresh work and endeavor. - Isaac Watts

Name _____

Message _____

_____

_____

Email / Phone _____

Name _____

Message _____

_____

_____

Email / Phone _____

Name _____

Message _____

_____

_____

Email / Phone _____

And in the end, it's not the years in your life that count. It's the life in your years.
- Abraham Lincoln

Name _____

Message _____

_____

_____

Email / Phone _____

Name _____

Message _____

_____

_____

Email / Phone _____

Name _____

Message _____

_____

_____

Email / Phone _____

> **I am long on ideas, but short on time. I expect to live to be only about a hundred.**
> **- Thomas Edison**

Name _____

Message _____

_____

_____

Email / Phone _____

Name _____

Message _____

_____

_____

Email / Phone _____

Name _____

Message _____

_____

_____

Email / Phone _____

Your life is a gift from the creator. Your gift back to the creator is what you do with your life.   - Billy Mills

Name _____

Message _____

_____

_____

Email / Phone _____

Name _____

Message _____

_____

_____

Email / Phone _____

Name _____

Message _____

_____

_____

Email / Phone _____

We turn not older with years but newer every day.
- Emily Dickinson

Name _____

Message _____

_____

_____

Email / Phone _____

Name _____

Message _____

_____

_____

Email / Phone _____

Name _____

Message _____

_____

_____

Email / Phone _____

The more you praise and celebrate your life, the more there is to celebrate.
_ Oprah Winfrey

Name _____

Message _____

_____

_____

Email / Phone _____

Name _____

Message _____

_____

_____

Email / Phone _____

Name _____

Message _____

_____

_____

Email / Phone _____

Whatever with the past has gone, the best is yet to come.
-Lucy Larcom

Name _____

Message _____

_____

_____

Email / Phone _____

Name _____

Message _____

_____

_____

Email / Phone _____

Name _____

Message _____

_____

_____

Email / Phone _____

Life is a gift. Never forget to enjoy and bask in every moment you are in.
—Unknown

Name _____

Message _____

_____

_____

Email / Phone _____

Name _____

Message _____

_____

_____

Email / Phone _____

Name _____

Message _____

_____

_____

Email / Phone _____

Life is not measured by the number of breaths we take, but by the moments that take our breath away. —George Carlin

Name _____

Message _____

_____

_____

Email / Phone _____

Name _____

Message _____

_____

_____

Email / Phone _____

Name _____

Message _____

_____

_____

Email / Phone _____

To know how to grow old is the master-work of wisdom, and one of the most difficult chapters is the great art of living.   -Henri Frederic Amiel

Name _____

Message _____

_____

_____

Email / Phone _____

Name _____

Message _____

_____

_____

Email / Phone _____

Name _____

Message _____

_____

_____

Email / Phone _____

Life isn't about finding yourself. Life is about creating yourself.
-George Bernard Shaw

Name _____

Message _____

_____

_____

Email / Phone _____

Name _____

Message _____

_____

_____

Email / Phone _____

Name _____

Message _____

_____

_____

Email / Phone _____

I have found that if you love life, life will love you back.
-Arthur Rubinstein

Name _____

Message _____

_____

_____

Email / Phone _____

Name _____

Message _____

_____

_____

Email / Phone _____

Name _____

Message _____

_____

_____

Email / Phone _____

It is our during darkness moments that we must focus to see the light.
-Aristotle Onassis

Name _____

Message _____

_____

_____

Email / Phone _____

Name _____

Message _____

_____

_____

Email / Phone _____

Name _____

Message _____

_____

_____

Email / Phone _____

Let your light shine. Shine within you so that it can shine on someone else. Let your light shine. –Oprah Winfrey

Name _____

Message _____

_____

_____

Email / Phone _____

Name _____

Message _____

_____

_____

Email / Phone _____

Name _____

Message _____

_____

_____

Email / Phone _____

If you do not hope, you will not find what is beyond your hopes.
- St. Clement of Alexandra

Name _____

Message _____

_____

_____

Email / Phone _____

Name _____

Message _____

_____

_____

Email / Phone _____

Name _____

Message _____

_____

_____

Email / Phone _____

You are as young as your faith, as old as your doubt, as young as your self-confidence, as old as your fear, as young as your hope, as old as your despair.
- Paul H. Duhn

Name _____

Message _____

_____

_____

Email / Phone _____

Name _____

Message _____

_____

_____

Email / Phone _____

Name _____

Message _____

_____

_____

Email / Phone _____

A birthday is a time to reflect on the year gone by, but to also set your goals for the upcoming year. -Catherine Pulsifer

Name _____

Message _____

_____

_____

Email / Phone _____

Name _____

Message _____

_____

_____

Email / Phone _____

Name _____

Message _____

_____

_____

Email / Phone _____

To know how to grow old is the master work of wisdom, and one of the most difficult chapters in the great art of living. *—Henri Frederic Amiel*

Name _____

Message _____

_____

_____

Email / Phone _____

Name _____

Message _____

_____

_____

Email / Phone _____

Name _____

Message _____

_____

_____

Email / Phone _____

Grow old along with me! The best is yet to be.
-Robert Browning

Name _____

Message _____

_____

_____

Email / Phone _____

Name _____

Message _____

_____

_____

Email / Phone _____

Name _____

Message _____

_____

_____

Email / Phone _____

Your past is not your potential. In any hour you can choose to liberate the future.
-Marilyn Ferguson

Name _____

Message _____

_____

_____

Email / Phone _____

Name _____

Message _____

_____

_____

Email / Phone _____

Name _____

Message _____

_____

_____

Email / Phone _____

Our birthdays are feathers in broad wing of time.
- Jean Paul Richter

Name _____

Message _____

_____

_____

Email / Phone _____

Name _____

Message _____

_____

_____

Email / Phone _____

Name _____

Message _____

_____

_____

Email / Phone _____

Don't just count your years, make your years count.
-Ernest Meyers

Name _____

Message _____

_____

_____

Email / Phone _____

Name _____

Message _____

_____

_____

Email / Phone _____

Name _____

Message _____

_____

_____

Email / Phone _____

Age is strictly a case of mind over matter. If you don't mind, it doesn't matter.
- Jack Benny

Name _____

Message _____

_____

_____

Email / Phone _____

Name _____

Message _____

_____

_____

Email / Phone _____

Name _____

Message _____

_____

_____

Email / Phone _____

Whatever with the past has gone, the best is always yet to come.
- Lucy Larcom

Name _____

Message _____

_____

_____

Email / Phone _____

Name _____

Message _____

_____

_____

Email / Phone _____

Name _____

Message _____

_____

_____

Email / Phone _____

A birthday is a time to reflect on the year gone by, but to also set your goals for the upcoming year. --*Catherine Pulsifer*

Name _____

Message _____

_____

_____

Email / Phone _____

Name _____

Message _____

_____

_____

Email / Phone _____

Name _____

Message _____

_____

_____

Email / Phone _____

You are never too old to set another goal or to dream a new dream.
-Les Brown

Name _____

Message _____

_____

_____

Email / Phone _____

Name _____

Message _____

_____

_____

Email / Phone _____

Name _____

Message _____

_____

_____

Email / Phone _____

When you were born, you cried and the world rejoiced. Live your life so that when you die, the world cries and you rejoice. *- Cherokee Expression*

Name _____

Message _____

_____

_____

Email / Phone _____

Name _____

Message _____

_____

_____

Email / Phone _____

Name _____

Message _____

_____

_____

Email / Phone _____

May you live all days of your life.
- Jonathan Swift

Name _____

Message _____

_____

_____

Email / Phone _____

Name _____

Message _____

_____

_____

Email / Phone _____

Name _____

Message _____

_____

_____

Email / Phone _____

Everyday is a birthday; every moment of it is new to us; we are born again, renewed for fresh work and endeavor. - Isaac Watts

Name _____

Message _____

_____

_____

Email / Phone _____

Name _____

Message _____

_____

_____

Email / Phone _____

Name _____

Message _____

_____

_____

Email / Phone _____

And in the end, it's not the years in your life that count. It's the life in your years.
- Abraham Lincoln

Name _____

Message _____

_____

_____

Email / Phone _____

Name _____

Message _____

_____

_____

Email / Phone _____

Name _____

Message _____

_____

_____

Email / Phone _____

I am long on ideas, but short on time. I expect to live to be only about a hundred.
- Thomas Edison

Name _____

Message _____

_____

_____

Email / Phone _____

Name _____

Message _____

_____

_____

Email / Phone _____

Name _____

Message _____

_____

_____

Email / Phone _____

Your life is a gift from the creator. Your gift back to the creator is what you do with your life. - Billy Mills

Name _____

Message _____

_____

_____

Email / Phone _____

Name _____

Message _____

_____

_____

Email / Phone _____

Name _____

Message _____

_____

_____

Email / Phone _____

We turn not older with years but newer every day.
- Emily Dickinson

Name _____

Message _____

_____

_____

Email / Phone _____

Name _____

Message _____

_____

_____

Email / Phone _____

Name _____

Message _____

_____

_____

Email / Phone _____

The more you praise and celebrate your life, the more there is to to celebrate. _ *Oprah Winfrey*

Name _____

Message _____

_____

_____

Email / Phone _____

Name _____

Message _____

_____

_____

Email / Phone _____

Name _____

Message _____

_____

_____

Email / Phone _____

To know how to grow old is the master-work of wisdom, and one of the most difficult chapters is the great art of living. _*Henri Frederic Amiel*

Name _____

Message _____

_____

_____

Email / Phone _____

Name _____

Message _____

_____

_____

Email / Phone _____

Name _____

Message _____

_____

_____

Email / Phone _____

As you grow older, may you grow richer in all of the most important things in life.
- Unknown

Name _____

Message _____

_____

_____

Email / Phone _____

Name _____

Message _____

_____

_____

Email / Phone _____

Name _____

Message _____

_____

_____

Email / Phone _____

Your past is not your potential. In any hour you can choose to liberate the future.
- Marilyn Ferguson

Name _____

Message _____

_____

_____

Email / Phone _____

Name _____

Message _____

_____

_____

Email / Phone _____

Name _____

Message _____

_____

_____

Email / Phone _____

To keep the heart unwrinkled, to be hopeful, kindly, cheerful, reverent that is triumph our old age. *—Thomas H. Aldrich*

Name _____

Message _____

_____

_____

Email / Phone _____

Name _____

Message _____

_____

_____

Email / Phone _____

Name _____

Message _____

_____

_____

Email / Phone _____

Aging is not lost youth but a new stage of opportunity and strength.
- Betty Friedan

Name _____

Message _____

_____

_____

Email / Phone _____

Name _____

Message _____

_____

_____

Email / Phone _____

Name _____

Message _____

_____

_____

Email / Phone _____

It takes courage to grow up and be who you really are.
- E.E. Cummings

Name _____

Message _____

_____

_____

Email / Phone _____

Name _____

Message _____

_____

_____

Email / Phone _____

Name _____

Message _____

_____

_____

Email / Phone _____

Your past is not your potential. In any hour you can choose to liberate the future.
- Marilyn Ferguson

Name _____

Message _____

_____

_____

Email / Phone _____

Name _____

Message _____

_____

_____

Email / Phone _____

Name _____

Message _____

_____

_____

Email / Phone _____

God give us the gift of life; it is up to us to give ourselves the gift of living well.
-Voltaire

Name _____

Message _____

_____

_____

Email / Phone _____

Name _____

Message _____

_____

_____

Email / Phone _____

Name _____

Message _____

_____

_____

Email / Phone _____

The more you praise and celebrate your life, the more there is in life to celebrate.
-Oprah Winfrey

Name _____

Message _____

_____

_____

Email / Phone _____

Name _____

Message _____

_____

_____

Email / Phone _____

Name _____

Message _____

_____

_____

Email / Phone _____

You are never too old to set another goal or to dream a new dream.
-Les Brown

Name _____

Message _____

_____

_____

Email / Phone _____

Name _____

Message _____

_____

_____

Email / Phone _____

Name _____

Message _____

_____

_____

Email / Phone _____

When you were born, you cried and the world rejoiced. Live your life so that when you die, the world cries and you rejoice. - *Cherokee Expression*

Name _____

Message _____

_____

_____

Email / Phone _____

Name _____

Message _____

_____

_____

Email / Phone _____

Name _____

Message _____

_____

_____

Email / Phone _____

May you live all days of your life.
- Jonathan Swift

Name _____

Message _____

_____

_____

Email / Phone _____

Name _____

Message _____

_____

_____

Email / Phone _____

Name _____

Message _____

_____

_____

Email / Phone _____

Success is like reaching an important birthday and finding you are exactly the same. - *Audrey Hepburn*

Name _____

Message _____

_____

_____

Email / Phone _____

Name _____

Message _____

_____

_____

Email / Phone _____

Name _____

Message _____

_____

_____

Email / Phone _____

And in the end, it's not the years in your life that count. It's the life in your years.
- Abraham Lincoln

Name _____

Message _____

_____

_____

Email / Phone _____

Name _____

Message _____

_____

_____

Email / Phone _____

Name _____

Message _____

_____

_____

Email / Phone _____

I am long on ideas, but short on time. I expect to live to be only about a hundred.
- Thomas Edison

Name _____

Message _____

_____

_____

Email / Phone _____

Name _____

Message _____

_____

_____

Email / Phone _____

Name _____

Message _____

_____

_____

Email / Phone _____

A diplomat is a man who always remembers a woman's birthday but never remembers her age.   - Robert Frost

Name _____

Message _____

_____

_____

Email / Phone _____

Name _____

Message _____

_____

_____

Email / Phone _____

Name _____

Message _____

_____

_____

Email / Phone _____

We turn not older with years but newer every day.
- Emily Dickinson

Name _____

Message _____

_____

_____

Email / Phone _____

Name _____

Message _____

_____

_____

Email / Phone _____

Name _____

Message _____

_____

_____

Email / Phone _____

The day which we fear as our last is but the birthday of eternity.
- Lucius Annaeus Seneca

Name _____

Message _____

_____

_____

Email / Phone _____

Name _____

Message _____

_____

_____

Email / Phone _____

Name _____

Message _____

_____

_____

Email / Phone _____

Whatever with the past has gone, the best is yet to come.
-Lucy Larcom

Name _____

Message _____

_____

_____

Email / Phone _____

Name _____

Message _____

_____

_____

Email / Phone _____

Name _____

Message _____

_____

_____

Email / Phone _____

Life is a gift. Never forget to enjoy and bask in every moment you are in.
—Unknown

Name _____

Message _____

_____

_____

Email / Phone _____

Name _____

Message _____

_____

_____

Email / Phone _____

Name _____

Message _____

_____

_____

Email / Phone _____

Life is not measured by the number of breaths we take, but by the moments that take our breath away.   –George Carlin

Name _____

Message _____

_____

_____

Email / Phone _____

Name _____

Message _____

_____

_____

Email / Phone _____

Name _____

Message _____

_____

_____

Email / Phone _____

To know how to grow old is the master-work of wisdom, and one of the most difficult chapters is the great art of living. *-Henri Frederic Amiel*

Name _____

Message _____

_____

_____

Email / Phone _____

Name _____

Message _____

_____

_____

Email / Phone _____

Name _____

Message _____

_____

_____

Email / Phone _____

Life isn't about finding yourself. Life is about creating yourself.
-George Bernard Shaw

Name _____

Message _____

_____

_____

Email / Phone _____

Name _____

Message _____

_____

_____

Email / Phone _____

Name _____

Message _____

_____

_____

Email / Phone _____

My policy on cake is pro having it and pro eating it
- Boris Johnson

Name _____

Message _____

_____

_____

Email / Phone _____

Name _____

Message _____

_____

_____

Email / Phone _____

Name _____

Message _____

_____

_____

Email / Phone _____

It is our during darkness moments that we must focus to see the light.
–Aristotle Onassis

Name _____

Message _____

_____

_____

Email / Phone _____

Name _____

Message _____

_____

_____

Email / Phone _____

Name _____

Message _____

_____

_____

Email / Phone _____

Let your light shine. Shine within you so that it can shine on someone else. Let your light shine. –Oprah Winfrey

Gift Log

DATE	GIFT DESCRIPTION	GIVEN BY	THANK YOU NOTICE SENT

Gift Log

DATE	GIFT DESCRIPTION	GIVEN BY	THANK YOU NOTICE SENT

Gift Log

DATE	GIFT DESCRIPTION	GIVEN BY	THANK YOU NOTICE SENT

Gift Log

DATE	GIFT DESCRIPTION	GIVEN BY	THANK YOU NOTICE SENT

Gift Log

DATE	GIFT DESCRIPTION	GIVEN BY	THANK YOU NOTICE SENT

Gift Log

DATE	GIFT DESCRIPTION	GIVEN BY	THANK YOU NOTICE SENT

Printed in Great Britain
by Amazon

Woodturning Tips
& Techniques

what woodturners need to know

Woodturning Tips
& Techniques

what woodturners need to know

Carol Rix

GUILD OF MASTER CRAFTSMAN PUBLICATIONS LTD

First published 2006 by
Guild of Master Craftsman Publications Ltd, 166 High Street, Lewes,
East Sussex BN7 1XU

Text © Carol Rix, 2006
Copyright in the Work © Guild of Master Craftsman Publications Ltd, 2006

Principal photography by Carol Rix ©. For other photographic credits see page 190.

Front cover (spine): photograph of pumpkin pot by Lee-Ann Wilson. Back cover: starfish (top) by Andrew Potocnik.

ISBN-13 978-1-86108-439-2
ISBN-10 1-86108-439-0

A catalogue record of this book is available from the British Library.

Production Manager: Hilary MacCallum
Managing Editor: Gerrie Purcell
Editor: Rachel Netherwood
Managing Art Editor: Gilda Pacitti
Design: Fineline Studios

Typeface: Meta Plus
Colour origination: Altaimage
Printed and bound: Sino Publishing

Measurements notice
Imperial measurements are conversions from metric;
they have been rounded up or down to the nearest 1/4, 1/2 or whole inch.

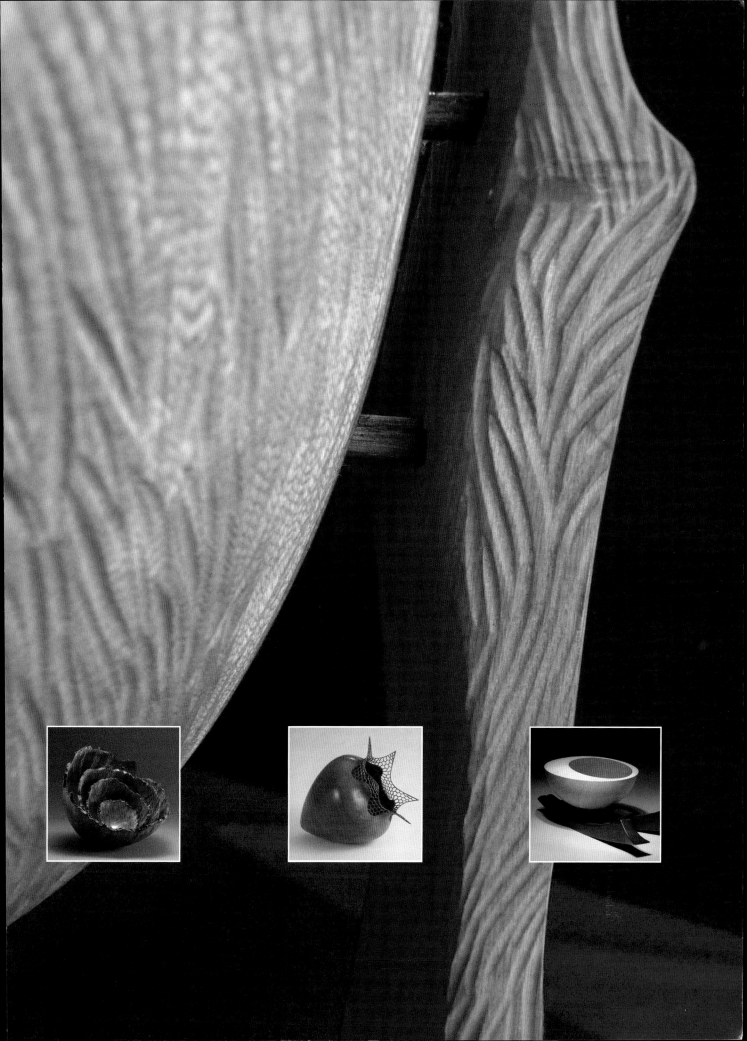

Contents

Part Three
Advanced Techniques

Woodturning and writing are two of my greatest passions. For quite a few years, I have been turning professionally and writing articles for an Australian woodworking magazine. It had seemed only logical that I should want to write a book about woodturning. However, the advice I received from local publishers and people who had 'been there and done that' was short and sharp: 'Don't.' Then came explanations revolving around the phrases, 'lots of work'; 'high risks'; 'small market'; 'poor returns' and so on. It seemed that the usual path was not the way to go and, for a while, I shelved the idea.

When my son, Graham, embarked on a new career in internet marketing he proposed that I, with this dream woodturning book in my head, become his guinea pig. He wanted to conduct some internet research to find out what it was about woodturning that people wanted to know. He then posted up a one-page site with my name on it, asking people for their questions: the most important questions that they had about woodturning. These questions were to provide the basis for the contents of the book that Graham was committing me to. In that month, around eighty people from all over the world responded with their questions. It was exciting receiving questions and good wishes from people who shared my interest in woodturning. There were some common themes running through a lot of the questions – things like sharpening, tool control, finishes and acquiring and drying wood. There was also a great range of other topics to be addressed.

The earliest chapters in the book are written for those people who are getting started and need to know about the machinery, the tools to buy, and how to set up a workshop. Chapters five to ten cover techniques for sharpening and using the tools; collecting, seasoning and storing the wood; and using the finishes. The later chapters are written for those people who have been turning for a while and wish to take it further.

Writing this book has been a growing experience for me. I hope you enjoy reading it as much as I have enjoyed putting it together.

Carol Rix

Part One

Setting Up

1

The Lathe

Buying a new or second-hand lathe

When you are first setting up a turning workshop, the obvious start is to look at lathes. Prices for these vary considerably and, generally speaking, you will get what you pay for. The cheaper lathes will be cheaper because the manufacturers have cut costs. They may have used rolled steel rather than cast iron, and overall the construction and accessories will tend to be flimsier.

Before deciding on the lathe for your workshop, decide on a price range and compare the lathes available within that range. To determine what is and isn't a good lathe, look for the features listed below and talk to a number of turners about what they consider important in a lathe. (If you aren't familiar with any of the terms used, refer to the glossary on pages 184–187.) If possible, get an experienced turner to go along with you when you look at a potential purchase.

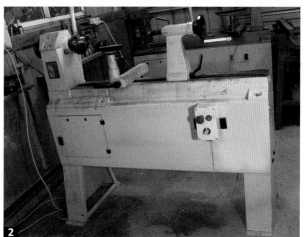

What to look for

1 Heavy duty construction: preferably a solid, cast iron bed as this is less likely to warp; and a solid, heavy stand sitting squarely on the floor. Some lathes have provision for slight adjustment of the feet to allow for floors that might not be flat.

1–**3** These lathes feature solid, cast iron beds and heavy duty stands. The lathes in **1** and **2** have deep beds to enable the turner to swing large pieces. The red bar along the front of lathe **1** is an emergency stopping bar – a useful safety feature. In **2**, the motor and belt pulleys are mounted on a hinged plate under the headstock and are easily accessible through the hinged door. The controls are also easily accessible, yet safely away from the spinning wood. Lathe **3** is cheaper, but still features a cast iron bed and stand. The wooden platform was added by the owner.

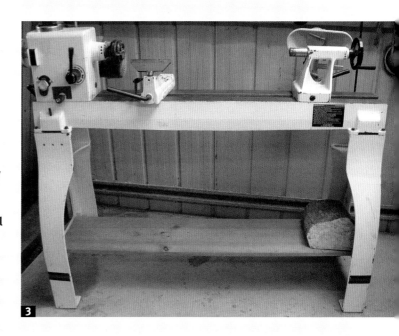

◀ The top of the headstock housing on this lathe lifts up to reveal the belt and drive pulleys. The belt is wide and grooved underneath to ensure it runs true on the pulleys. Speeds are shown on the plate on the front of the housing.

To ensure that they line up properly, put the headstock and tailstock points in and bring the tailstock up until the points just touch. You can also check this by drilling with a twist drill in a Jacob's chuck mounted in the tailstock. The drill should enter the spinning wood at the centre. If it has to jump sideways slightly as it enters the wood, then the points may not be lined up correctly.

2 Solid, stable motor mountings.

3 Quiet operation: the motor must run smoothly; there should be no bearing noise or vibration at any speed or with any reasonable load.

4 The belt should run smoothly and it should be easy to change speeds. Check that the belt does not jump or flex when running. Is it easy to see what speed the lathe is set on before you start up?

5 The tailstock and tool rest banjo should slide freely for the full length of the lathe bed.

6 Headstock and tailstock points should line up.

7 The levers to change the position of the tool rest and tailstock should be easy to get at and easy to adjust – cam lock systems are best.

View of a cam lock system on a tailstock assembly. Slight movement of the lever will raise the disc and lock it against the bottom of the bed. This is quick and easy.

> **▶** Indexing system: the small wheel at the bottom is attached to a spring-loaded pin through the housing. Turn the wheel and it will lock into the small bar beside it. The pin locks into one of 24 numbered holes on the pulley. Other systems have up to 144 or more stop points. The indexing system enables accurate spacing of drill holes or routing around the outside of spindle and faceplate work.

8 Indexing system should be present, easy to see and use and have at least 24 positions.

9 All accessories should be present and in good condition. There should be at least one tool rest (preferably two – a short and a long one); a faceplate; drive spur for the headstock (make sure the point and spur are not bent or damaged); knockout bar; live tailstock centre (one that spins), and check to see that the point is sharp and the bearings aren't worn or noisy.

10 Some extra bonuses:
– Variable speed – some even have reverse, which is good for hollowing and sanding difficult, torn grain
– A four-jaw expanding chuck to fit the lathe
– A movable light
– Storage shelves built into the stand

⌃ Accessories from left to right: headstock spur drive; cone with removable tip (handy if you want to drill into spindle work, such as when making lamp stands); small tailstock point; large live tailstock point; and cup.

Accessories: faceplates are useful in both sizes. I have drilled extra holes in each one to enable screws for solid gripping, especially when off-centre work is being done.

The knockout bar is used for knocking out headstock and tailstock centres so that a faceplate, chuck or Jacob's chuck can be used.

16

Buying or constructing a lathe stand

Whether you buy or construct your own lathe stand will depend on a number of factors: whether your lathe comes with its own integral stand; the cost of the stand and your own budget constraints; your own woodworking or metal working construction abilities; and the time you have available.

Whether you buy or build your lathe stand, it is most important that it is solid and stable. You do not want the lathe and its stand to start vibrating across the floor as soon as you put on something that is a bit off-balance.

A flimsy stand is often one feature of the cheaper lathes that the buyer needs to beware of. (If you already have a flimsy, commercially produced lathe stand, some of the suggestions here could be adapted to make the stand more solid and user-friendly.)

Since there are so many different lathes on the market, there is no point including plans for a lathe stand here. However, if you wish to design and build your own stand, you could consider some of the following features.

1–**2** This home-made lathe stand is simple but solid. Note the footing blocks, which extend along the floor past the width of the lathe itself. This is to make the whole assembly more stable. A cage has been constructed in front of the lathe to protect the operator of the lathe in front from any possible mishaps. The motor is mounted directly under the headstock on a hinged wooden platform. Pressing down on the green lever in **2** raises the platform to allow changing of the belt to adjust speeds. The switch could have been located in a safer position towards the tailstock. As it is, if a piece of wood comes loose on the lathe, the operator has to lean in the danger path to switch off the lathe.

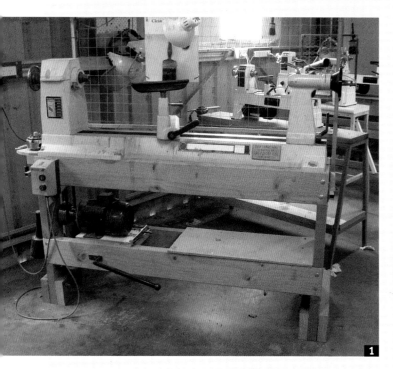

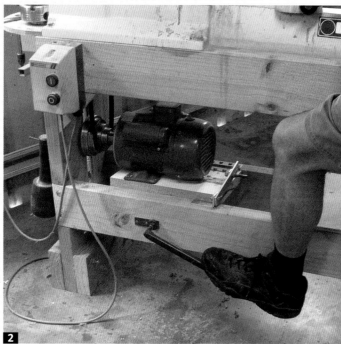

1   **2**

3 shows the front view and **4** shows the back of a trapezoidal box construction lathe stand. **4** illustrates the hole through which sand can be poured to give the lathe extra weight and stability. If necessary the sand can be emptied out through a hole at the bottom.

- The lathe could be made solid by use of heavy metal or large section framing timbers (see **1**–**2**).

- Some lathe stands are constructed with a section of the top of the stand sloping away, so that shavings and dust are deflected away from the stand and the operator. This is useful, but only if you can get behind the lathe to clean up later.

- The section under the lathe bed could be constructed with built-in shelves and/or drawers to house all your lathe accessories.

- The ends of the frame could be trapezoidal so that the feet of the lathe are much wider than the lathe itself. One way of making a home-made lathe stand more solid is to build both ends approximately 3in (76mm) thick using box construction techniques and cover with five-ply plywood. Drill large holes at the tops and bottoms of each end and cut or turn plugs or plates that can later be screwed over the holes. Once the lathe is mounted and in place in the workshop and you are satisfied with its position, uncover the holes at the top of each end and pour dry sand into the hollow. With that extra weight, the lathe shouldn't go anywhere. If you do need to move the lathe, you can empty the sand out by uncovering the hole at the bottom.

18

■ Consider your own height when constructing your lathe stand. Once mounted on the stand, the lathe centre should be roughly at elbow height or a bit above.

■ The stand could have an extension or ledge on one end or at the back with fittings and holes to keep accessories and tools.

■ The stand for a small, portable lathe could have handles on one end and wheels at the other.

⌃ Accessory ledge with places for knockout bar, faceplate, chuck, Jacob's chuck, screw chuck, drive centre and tailstock centre.

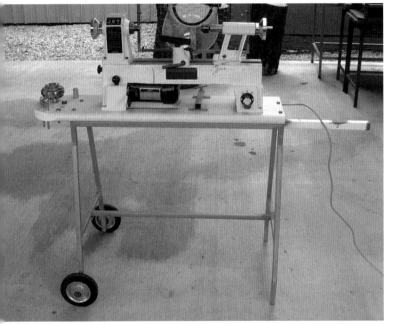

These two stands, designed for small, portable lathes, have some good features. They are themselves very portable; all tools and accessories are stored in view and close at hand; the handle on the metal stand can be hinged out of the way when not in use; and the wooden stand is also a great little storage unit. However, both could do with some improvements. The wheels tend to be a bit flimsy and make the stands unstable – more so with the wooden one because the legs aren't splayed. This could be overcome by including fold-down, lock-in feet in front of or beside the wheels. Facility for a light, drop-in wire screen (for safety at the front of the lathe) could also be included.

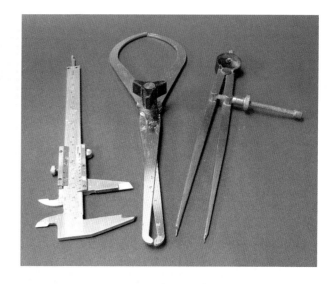

▶ Measuring tools from left to right: vernier callipers for accurately measuring widths on spindle work; inside-outside callipers for measuring the thickness of a bowl or vessel wall; dividers.

Lathe accessories

There are some lathe accessories that come as part of the lathe: the drive centre for the headstock and tailstock centre; at least one faceplate; and a knockout bar to knock out the drive centres when they are not needed.

Other lathe accessories, which should enable a greater range of turning projects, have to be purchased separately. These include measuring tools, four-jaw expanding chucks, Jacob's chuck, a movable light and a steady rest. The latter, although not essential, does come in handy to support long spindle work or work which is being hollowed a long way from the supporting chuck.

A range of four-jaw expanding chucks with some of the different jaws available, from left to right: Nova chuck with standard jaws (top left), screw chuck with home-made washer, C and straight bar for adjusting the jaw opening and shark jaws and Allen key; VM 90 chuck fitted with long nose jaws (top centre), pin jaws, inserts to fit different screw threads on lathes and bars for adjusting jaw width; VM 120 chuck with standard jaws (top right), wide dovetail jaws, bars and Allen key and shark jaws.

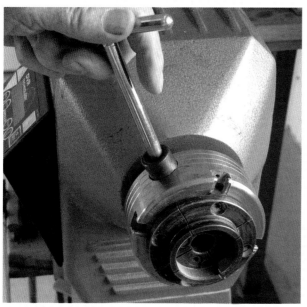

◀ The supernova chuck with T-bar tightening system. Tightening of the chuck jaws can be done one-handed, leaving the other hand free to hold the wood steady. One chuck with standard jaws is quite adequate for the beginner just setting up.

20

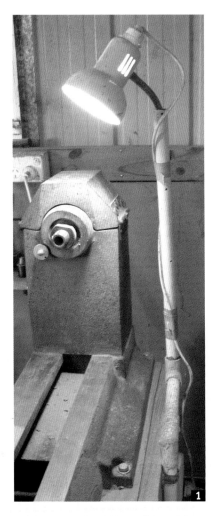

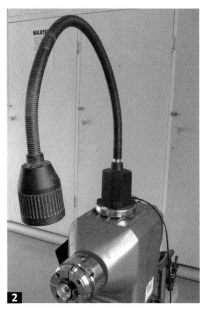

Good, adjustable lighting is essential if you are to get a good finish on your work. The home-made adjustable light in **1** is made from polythene piping, a couple of brackets and an old bedside light. **2** shows a commercially available, long gooseneck halogen lamp with a magnetic base. The light in **3** is screwed onto an old magnetic speaker so that it sits firmly on the headstock.

Jacob's chuck, for drilling on the lathe. The tapering stem fits into both the headstock and the tailstock. This one is a number 2 Morse taper, the most common size. Some older, smaller lathes used to come with a number 1 Morse taper, which is much thinner. These aren't very common now.

A three-point steady rest is used to hold long work which is being hollowed a long way from its support on the headstock. This is a bonus, but not essential when starting out.

2

The Bench Grinder

22

After the lathe and chisels, the bench grinder is the next most important piece of equipment for the turner. It is needed to shape and sharpen tools and it should be set up close to the lathe (unless the turner wants some exercise), with good lighting.

Wet and dry grinders

The most common type of grinder on the market is the dry grinder, which usually comes with 6 or 8in (150 or 205mm) wheels. The former is recommended for turners (although there is some debate over this), as the peripheral speed on the latter will be greater and more likely to burn the tools. The 8in grinder also gives a shallower hollow grind (more on that later).

The grinders usually come with two wheels – one coarse and one fine. For the finer grit wheel, which will be used more frequently for sharpening, a white, 80- or 120-grit aluminium oxide wheel, designed for sharpening high-speed steel tools, is recommended. The wheels rotate in a clockwise direction so that they are spinning downwards towards the tool as it is resting on the tool rest. The sharpening instructions here are based on this type of grinder. The grinding wheels rotate at approximately 3,000 rpm. At this speed, sharpening tools is a fairly quick process. However, there is always the danger of the thin tool edge overheating and turning blue. Once this happens, the steel has lost its temper and it will not hold its sharp edge.

Taking this into account, there are on the market wet stone grinders that rotate in an anticlockwise direction at a much slower speed. The wheels are wider and they pass through a bath of water as they rotate. Some accessories such as holding jigs, angle guides and grinding paste come with the grinder. Because of the slower speed and the constant wetting, these grinders solve the problem of overheating and they produce a nice, sharp edge. However, they are much slower to use and are considerably more expensive than the standard dry grinder.

One of a range of wet stone grinders on the market. The wheel is rotating away from the operator and passes through the water bath underneath. The tool rest or holding jig is attached to the bar above the wheel. The second, darker wheel is a leather strop.

Grinding jigs

There are lots of different grinding/sharpening jigs available and I have come across many turners who swear by the excellence of the jig that they have. Most of these jigs replace the tool rest in front of the grinding wheel and consist of an extendable bar and cradle or socket arrangement mounted directly under the wheel, and a holding mechanism that the tool is clamped into and which pivots in the cradle. The grinding angle on the tool can be set and maintained by adjusting the length of the extendable bar. The ones I have used usually do produce a nice, evenly ground hollow bevel and a good, sharp edge. (The even grind is the hardest thing for the beginner to achieve, especially on skew chisels and gouges.)

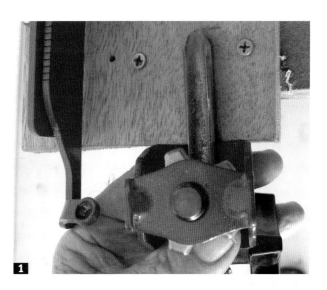

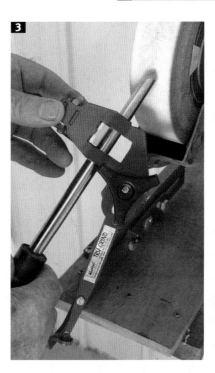

The Tru-Grind sharpening jig in action. Note the extendable bar under the grinder, which is set to produce the desired grinding angle. The angle of the bevel is maintained by initially setting the position of the gouge in the clamp, and then marking its length on the grinding stand. This mark acts as a positioning guide each time the gouge is re-sharpened **1**. When the gouge is clamped firmly in the holder **2**, the holder pivots in the socket below and in front of the grinding wheel **3**–**4**. Set right, the jig produces a nice, consistent, evenly ground bevel way down each side of the gouge. Note also, the wide, white aluminium oxide wheel in use. The face of the wheel is flat – being dressed regularly with a diamond dresser to keep it that way (see page 25).

An adjustable platform mounted in place of the tool rest. It has two adjustable pivot points – one at bench height and one under the platform.

However, I have experienced one problem with jigs being set up for my grinder. Because I have a range of tools of different shapes and lengths (some being very short or small), I have found that the jigs cannot accommodate all my tools. Without the tool rest on the grinder it becomes very inconvenient to get some of the shorter tools sharpened. My personal preference is to grind freehand. This does take a bit of practice at first, but once you gain confidence, it becomes a very quick and satisfying way to do it. When starting out, an old piece of pipe cut in half down some of its length and mounted on a handle can be used as a surrogate practice gouge. Other flat pieces of scrap steel can be made up like scrapers, parting tools and skew chisels. With these, you can practise all you like; it doesn't matter if you blue the metal and you won't be wasting good tool steel.

The standard tool rest that comes with the grinder is satisfactory for nearly all tools, except one: the skew chisel. For this tool the rest is not wide enough, because the skew needs to be held at angles to the stone to sharpen each side.

The adjustable platform set up with an angle guide to sharpen the skew chisel. Note that, for both sides, the top edge of the skew is parallel to the top of the table.

Therefore the skew is always in danger of falling off the sides of the rest. To solve this problem, I bought an adjustable platform that can be mounted on the bench in front of the grinder in place of the tool rest. This table can be set at the desired angle to get the right bevel on the skew and it is wide enough to support it. It does need to be of solid construction so that it doesn't flex or move once the angle is set and the tool is pressed hard against it for sharpening. The top

edge of the table can be used as a standard tool rest for freehand grinding of all the other tools.

Over time, the grinding wheel may wear unevenly and become clogged with dirt and steel dust. It needs periodic dressing to clean and true it up. With the wheel running, you either move the diamond tip across the wheel or simply press the T-bar dresser against the wheel face to take off the dirt and high points.

Build-up of dirt and steel dust means it is time for the wheel to be dressed.

Diamond dressers for truing up the face of the grinding wheel. I prefer the larger, T-bar dresser. It is much easier to get a flat, clean wheel with it.

3

The Workshop

If you are in the enviable position of having a new workshop area to furnish, some research into what others have done and some serious planning could save a lot of inconvenience further down the line. This chapter is intended to offer some ideas as to what tools other than a lathe and bench grinder are needed and how to set up a workshop that is easy to work in.

The band saw

Unless you can get a ready supply of prepared blanks, the band saw is a necessity. It is essential for preparation of stock: rough cutting logs for drying; cutting spindle blanks to length; and cutting circular bowl blanks. There are times when work done on the lathe also needs to be cut.

As with lathes, you get what you pay for. There are 'cheap' band saws on the market, but they are cheap because the manufacturer has cut corners by using less metal and second-rate materials. Buy a cheap model and you are looking at more broken blades, poor cutting performance, problems with tensioning, and stressed and broken parts later on.

Band saws come in a range of shapes and sizes. The most useful ones for the wood turner are either the stand-mounted or floor models. Bench-mounted band saws, especially the three-wheel versions, are too small to be of any great use.

The green stand-mounted band saw in **1** has been modified to store a cleaning brush in an obvious place and to take dust extraction. The most recent models have dust extraction facilities built in. The motor is housed in the bottom stand. This is the smallest practicable machine. The operator of the larger floor model in **2** is rip-sawing a log in preparation for spindle work. The wider blade on this saw will only cut straight. A narrower blade is necessary for cutting circles.

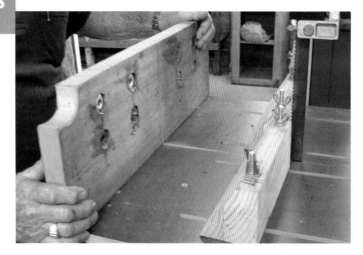

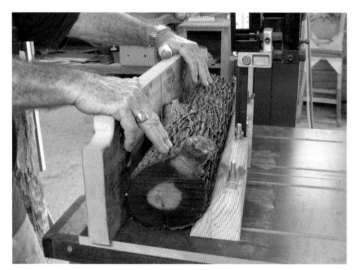

Learning to use a band saw is relatively easy. However, operating it safely requires constant safety consciousness. Don't persevere with a blunt blade. When the blade is blunt, you try to force the wood through, and accidents happen. Secondly, always make sure the wood is supported as it is being cut. Put a triangular chock under a log or round stock if you are going to cross cut it so that it doesn't roll into the blade. Better still, make a cradle or a holding jig to hold the wood steady. The stock to be cut must be pushed, not rolled through. If allowed to roll into the blade, the wood will catch and bend the blade. You must *never* hold the work with your hands in front of, or close to the blade.

Tip

There is a lot to learn about types of blades and tuning and maintaining the saw to get optimum performance out of it. The best book I have come across on this topic is *Band Saw Handbook* by Mark Duginske.

Safe use of the band saw, using jigs for holding logs or round stock to prevent them rolling into the blade and jamming or bending it. Keep hands clear of the blade at all times.

Hand tools

Other tools that come in handy include most of the general handyman pieces – a set of drill bits, a power hand drill, screws and screwdrivers, sandpaper, brushes, rags, hammer, mallet, spanners, gluing clamps and a roll of non-slip rubber matting.

Part of the work bench, holding bench grinders, mitre saw, vice and work in various stages of completion. With the shadow board behind, you know at a glance where everything is and what needs to be put away.

The work bench

The workbench is used for planning work, assembly of materials and for temporary storage of materials and tools for the current job. It can also be used for the mounting of a bench vice and the grinder. It should be large (you can never have enough bench space), solid, flat and level on top. The area underneath the bench can also be used for storage of materials or tools.

30

Ventilation and dust extraction

Your local climate will determine whether you have to consider heating or cooling for your workshop. Besides that, clean air is also essential.

For a workshop in a warm climate, consider designing it (if you have that luxury) with doors and windows opposite each other so there is an unrestricted passage of air through the building. Judiciously placed air vents and ceiling and wall fans could assist this. It all serves two purposes – cooling and dust extraction.

In cooler climates, or in a workshop enclosed under the house, where airflow is restricted, consider getting a ceiling-mounted air filter to suck up, filter and recycle the air in the room. There are a number of different sizes on the market.

You also need to consider setting up dust extraction for the band saw, lathe and other machinery. To reduce noise and to prevent tiny particles of dust being returned into the workshop atmosphere, the dust extractor should be located outside the workshop and ducting set up from the machinery to the extractor.

Storage of materials and tools

Planning good storage facilities for tools and other materials can make the difference between every job being a trial or a pleasure. While you are working on the lathe, your tools need to be close by, easily seen and held securely so that there is no danger of them falling on hard concrete, or worse still, soft feet. All other lathe accessories also need to have a visible spot close by the lathe. A shadow board on the wall next to the lathe or above the workbench is a good place to store hand tools so that they are easy to get to and easy to replace. For other materials, such as sandpaper, screws, power tools, glues and paints, a closed cupboard to exclude the dust is a good idea. Wood, unless it is going to be used soon, is best stored outside the work area (where there is less dust), and in a dry area where air can circulate freely (see chapter 6, 'The Wood').

◀ **Part of the ducting system for dust extraction. The dust extractor is housed in a separate annexe next to the shed. The power cord and ducts feed through the opening in the wall and the extractor is switched on inside the shed. You can have the extractor wired so that it switches on automatically once a machine is started up. The gates are opened or closed depending on which machine is being used.**

▶ **Some storage options for lathe tools. In 1, a shelf is attached on the wall next to the lathe. Holes are drilled through the shelf to drop tools into. Lathe accessories and jigs are stored on the wall above the tools. Another option is shown in 2 – a portable tool rack to be moved wherever it is needed.**

Safety

Finally, it is important to keep the workshop as safe as possible. It must be free from fire hazards, and be as uncluttered and dust free as possible. Keep guards on the machinery. Ensure a good circulation of clean air in the workshop and, while working on the lathe, a dust mask and face shield should be worn – better still, a full helmet respirator.

▼ Your eyes and face need to be protected from flying chips and, occasionally, an airborne turning. Ensure that you are breathing clean air. Dust can cause serious lung problems. Your skin also needs to be protected. Even on the hottest summer days, I now wear a long-sleeved shirt, buttoned up to the neck. I learned the hard way, that on a hot day, the pores of the skin open up and dust enters and irritates, causing skin rashes. This is definitely not pleasant!

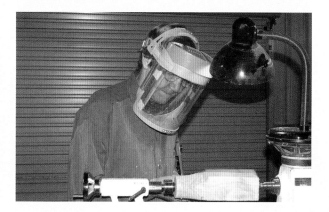

4

The Tools

Tools you need to get started

To start out, the beginner turner needs no more than six or seven tools: a roughing gouge or a large bowl gouge (often called a supa-gouge); a ⅜in (9.5mm) bowl gouge; a spindle or detail gouge (these have a much shallower flute than the bowl gouge and are best ground to a lady's fingernail shape); a parting tool; a skew chisel and a couple of scrapers (a flat nose and a round or half-round nose). Get the best high-speed steel tools your budget will allow. Cheap tools will give you plenty of sharpening practice, but not a lot of satisfaction on the lathe.

▶ From top to bottom: a square-section square end scraper (a heavy duty tool good for hollowing work); a 1in (25mm) square end scraper; a round nose scraper; two half-round or round-sided scrapers. Start with a square nose and a round nose scraper.

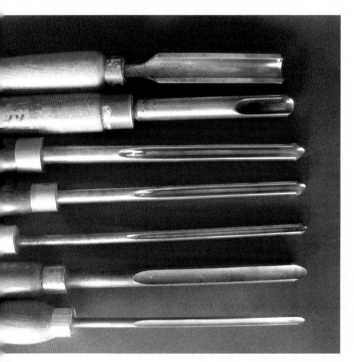

▼ The middle parting tool has a diamond-shaped profile to reduce the chance of the tool binding when parting a piece off. The bottom tool is a very thin tool, home-made from an old metal power hacksaw blade: this is useful when you haven't got a lot of material left for parting off.

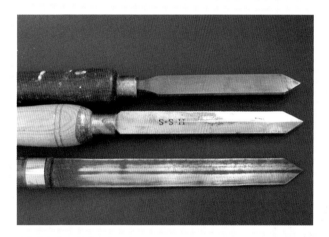

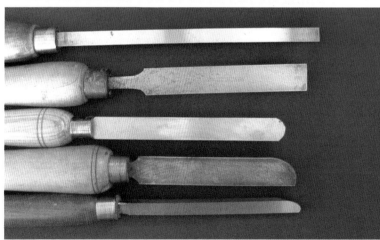

◀ From top to bottom: 1in (25mm) roughing gouge; ¾in (19mm) bowl gouge; ½in (13mm) bowl gouge; ⅜in (9.5mm) bowl gouge; ¼in (6mm) bowl gouge; ⅝in (16mm) detail gouge; ¼in (6mm) detail gouge. Note the much shallower flute on the detail gouges. To start with, the best ones to get would be the ¾in (19mm) bowl gouge, which does the same job as a roughing gouge and more; the ⅜in (9.5mm) bowl gouge and the ¼in (6mm) detail gouge.

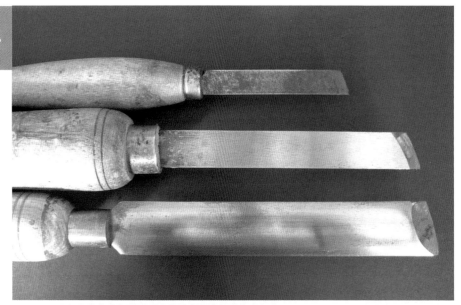

Skew chisels. The old carbon steel chisel (top) is good for the occasional tight spot, but not for frequent use. Most beginner turners prefer the standard flat-sided skew (middle). It is far more stable than the oval one (bottom) when used on its side. The sharp edges down the sides of the tool can be ground back slightly to reduce damage to the tool rest.

What tool does what job?

There is overlap between the tools that can be used to do a certain job. Where a gouge might be the most usual tool for a job, it might also be possible to use a skew chisel or a scraper. So, the descriptions here should be used as a guide only, to be tested and adopted or rejected as it suits. See also chapter 8, 'Using the tools' and the glossary on pages 184–187, as there are a lot of woodturning terms used here that the beginner may not be familiar with.

- ■ **Round nose scraper** This tool is most commonly used in faceplate or hollowing work. It can be used for rough turning, safely removing waste material. When the tool is sharp and the touch light, it is often used for finishing cuts in bowls and the inside of hollow vessels. It may also be used to make grooves and coves on spindle turnings, although the detail gouge makes a neater job of this.

Using the round nose scraper for final waste removal and cleaning up inside a bowl.

▶▶ Using a small, flat nose scraper ground at an angle to cut a shallow recess in the bottom of a wine bottle coaster. This was an old woodworking chisel.

■ **Square nose scraper** The uses to which the scraper can be put are determined very much by the size and thickness of the tool. The scraper can be used for fast removal of material in faceplate turnings, especially those with flat bottoms. More solid scrapers can be used safely for hollowing work. Square nose scrapers can also be used to smooth flat or convex surfaces such as the outside of a bowl.

■ **Parting tool** As its name suggests, this is used for parting off spindle work. It will also clean up end grain on spindle work; cut a spigot in end grain work, in preparation for gripping in a chuck; and it can be used to achieve a designated thickness in spindle work (see chapter 8, 'Using the tools').

Using a small square nose scraper to cut a flat base in a wine bottle coaster.

Using a parting tool to cut a spigot in preparation for work to be held in a chuck, to part off spindle work and to cut flat sections of a defined thickness.

Using the skew chisel to face off end grain and mark a groove before opening it up from both sides of the groove as a V-cut in spindle work.

Using the skew on its side to refine details and to execute a planing cut on spindle work. It produces a very clean cut.

■ **Skew chisel** When the long point is used, the skew is an excellent tool for facing off end grain. It is not as easy to use as the parting tool but does a cleaner job. It can be used for cutting grooves, tidying up fillets and sharp edges on spindle work and for parting off when a clean face is required on the parted piece. The bottom third of the flat edge can be used as a planing blade to produce a very smooth surface on straight spindle work. The short point can be used to cut and tidy up deep coves that are too narrow for a detail gouge to get into on spindle work. It can also be used to produce a peeling cut when forming a spigot to hold spindle work in a chuck, and to cut decorative grooves in faceplate work. Once mastered, it is a very versatile tool.

Executing a peeling cut on the end of spindle work to produce a spigot and cutting grooves in faceplate work with the skew.

Using the roughing gouge **1** and the large bowl gouge **2** to rough out spindle work.

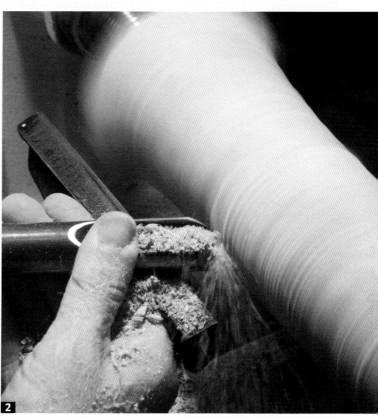

Using a large ¾in (9.5mm) detail gouge **1** and a smaller ¼in (6mm) detail gouge **2** to shape fine details on spindle work. The long fingernail grind and shallow flutes enable the detail gouge to get into smaller spaces than the bowl gouge.

- **Detail or spindle gouge** This tool is mostly used for doing fine detailed work, cutting beads, coves and fillets on spindle work. It is best for getting into fairly tight curves. The strength of detail gouges and spindle gouges lies in the 'lady's fingernail' grind that enables the turner to cut fine details primarily in spindle work. There is a certain amount of overlap between what the bowl gouge and the detail gouge will do and also what the detail gouge and the skew chisel will do. These gouges range in size from ¼in (6mm), which will only do very fine work, to ¾in (19mm), which is a very solid tool capable of some fine work, but also capable of doing considerable waste removal or roughing out.

- **Bowl gouge** When a roughing gouge is not available, a large bowl gouge – ½in (13mm) or larger – can be used to rough out stock. A ⅜in (9.5mm) bowl gouge is one of the most useful tools in your set. It can be used for shaping spindle work, but its main use is for turning bowls – both outside and inside.

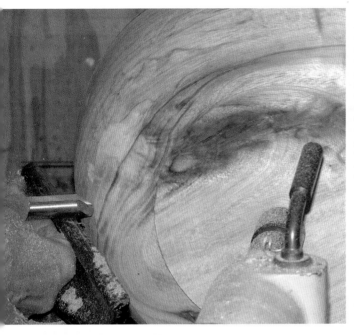

Using bowl gouges to rough out and shape the outside, the foot and the inside of a bowl.

Using bowl gouges to execute fine finishing cuts and face off the base of a wine coaster.

5
Sharpening

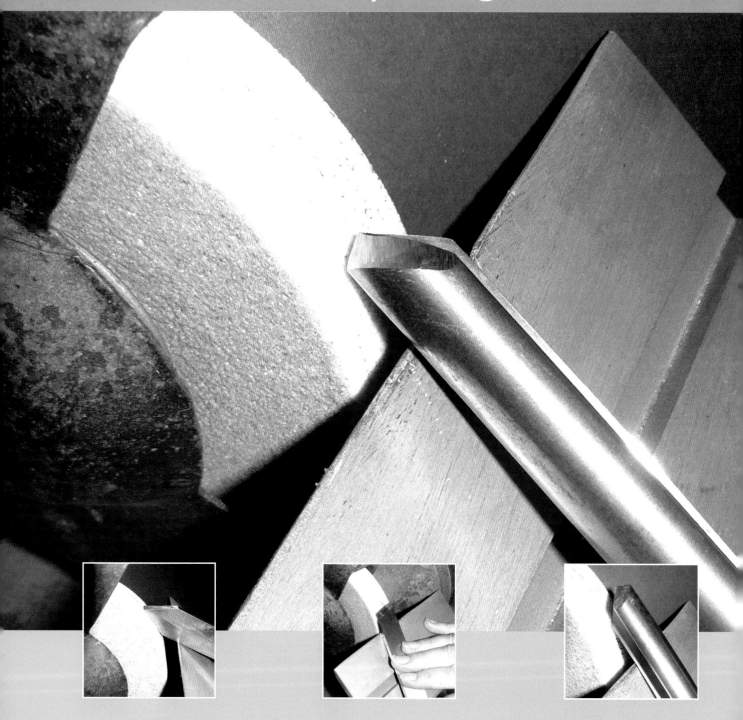

Grinding, sharpening and honing – some general principles

Sharpening tools is a topic about which every turner has their own opinion, so to write about the subject is to invite dissension. Some turners love using a particular grinding jig. Others prefer to sharpen freehand on the grinding wheel. Some turners prefer to hone frequently with a stone while others rarely hone, but use their tools straight from the grinding wheel. Some turners are happy to use the shaped grind on the tool as it comes from the manufacturers, while others insist on dramatically changing the grind on certain tools. And so on! What it boils down to is that each turner needs to develop his or her own grinds and sharpening techniques to suit.

However, there are some principles which the turner needs to be aware of before blithely going ahead and developing their own sharpening techniques.

Firstly, when you are grinding or sharpening a tool, you are not just getting a sharp edge on the end of the tool. You are also creating a bevel – the area of ground tool that is just behind the sharp edge. This bevel is just as important as the sharp edge itself. The bevel rests on the turning wood as it is being cut; it supports the tool, gives it stability and makes it possible to produce a nice, smooth cut.

On most tools, the bevel must be hollow-ground; that is, it must be concave in profile. This is so that it sits stable on the wood. A convex grind on the bevel will cause the tool to wobble and it won't cut cleanly. Hold the tool up side-on in front of your face and check to see that you do have that hollow grind. If, when you sharpen on the grindstone, you are grinding the whole of the bevel, the hollow grind will automatically be there. You will lose it if you only keep sharpening the tip of the tool and you will then end up with the unwanted convex shape. One way to check that you are sharpening the whole bevel is to draw over all of it with a coloured felt pen before putting it on the stone. Afterwards, check that you have removed all of the colour and that you have produced a smooth ground surface over the whole of the bevel.

1 A concave profile or hollow grind on a parting tool.

42

Secondly, the turner needs to be aware of the fact that there is a difference between grinding, sharpening and honing the tools. We grind away metal on the tools to get the profile that we want. Start with a fairly coarse stone and, when closer to the desired profile, change over to a finer stone (most commercial grinders come with the facility for at least two stones). Once the profile is established, we should rarely need to go back to the coarse stone. Sharpening is done on the finer stone (usually 120 grit; a white aluminium oxide stone is best for high-speed steel tools) when the tool starts to become blunt. It is only a quick touch-up – no more than one or two passes of the tool on the stone to restore the edge. Many turners find that this quick sharpening on the grindstone produces a satisfactory edge and go straight back to the lathe.

However, others prefer to go one step further and will hone their tools by hand on a finer grade whetstone or diamond-impregnated file. When done fairly frequently, this too can be a reasonably quick process and keeps the tool edge razor sharp. There are various schools of thought as to how honing should be carried out. Methods include rubbing the tool in a figure-of-eight on a water- or oil-lubricated whetstone; filing straight from the back end of the bevel towards the edge; filing straight from the edge backwards; filing backwards and forwards. Try each and see which one suits you. Tools last longer if they are fine honed rather than being taken to the grindstone each time.

Thirdly, when grinding or sharpening on a standard dry grinder, it is important to beware of overheating the tool. The rule is 'gently, gently': not too much pressure and not for too long. If the tool edge gets too hot and turns blue, it loses its temper and will not hold a sharp edge.

It has been common practice when grinding to have a tin of water next to the grinder to dunk and cool the tool at frequent intervals. This works for carbon steel tools, but can cause damage to the metal structure of high-speed steel tools.

Finally, it is important to sharpen or hone as soon as you feel that the tool is not cutting well, or that you seem to be putting more pressure on the tool to get results. Do not work with a blunt tool. It leads to inaccuracies and a rough finish.

At what angles should the tools be ground?

There are no hard-and-fast rules as to what angle the bevel should be ground; it will depend on the height of the turner in relation to the lathe and the angle at which you hold the tool when cutting. So, take the angles given in A–E as a guide only.

Grinding Angles

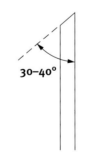

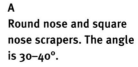

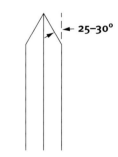

A
Round nose and square nose scrapers. The angle is 30–40°.

B
Parting tools. The angle should be about 25–30° on each side.

Sharpening each tool

When you first learn to sharpen, it is a good idea to mark the whole bevel with a felt pen before you put the tool to the stone. Doing this makes it possible, at a glance, to see where tool and stone have connected and where they haven't.

Square nose scraper

The square nose scraper is one of the easiest tools to sharpen. Start the grinder and bring the heel of the bevel (the bottom part) in contact with the wheel (see **2**).

Then, raise the handle of the tool until the whole bevel is in contact with the wheel, but no further. Sparks will fly over the edge in contact with the wheel. (See **3**.) Don't put heavy pressure on the tool against the wheel and don't hold the tool there too long. Keep the movement a fluid one; you don't want to cook the edge. Remember: gently, gently.

2–**3** Sharpening the square nose scraper.

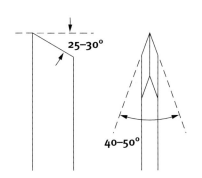

C
Skew chisels. The angle of the skew should be about 25–30°. The bevel angle should be about 40–50°.

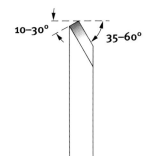

D
Bowl gouge. For a bowl gouge and roughing gouge, the bevel is around 20°. Too sharp a bevel will make the tool difficult to control. Most turners grind the bevel on a bowl gouge well along the tool sides (see page 47).

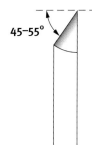

E
Detail gouges. The bevel on a spindle or detail gouge is much sharper than that of a bowl or roughing gouge as it is mostly used to produce fine, detailed spindle work.

44

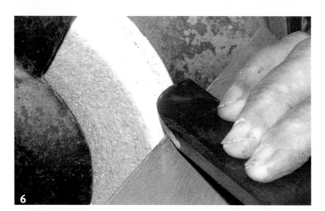

4 Sharpening the square nose scraper.

If the scraper is a wide one, then you may have to move the tool backwards and forwards across the face of the wheel to get the whole tool sharpened (see **4**).

Check to see that you have touched up the whole bevel. Also, look at the back of the sharp edge. If you see small indentations, shiny spots or unevenness along the edge, take it back to the wheel for a second go.

Round and half-round nose scrapers

The technique for sharpening the round or half-round nose scraper is very similar to that for the square nose scraper. However, instead of moving the tool directly across the grinding wheel once the whole bevel is in contact, you need to bring the tool round in a smooth arc. Where you start will depend on what is most comfortable for you. With the half-round scraper, my preference is to start on the side of the tool and then swing it around to the front (see **5**). Start the grinder, bring the heel of the tool up and raise the tool handle until the whole bevel is in contact with the wheel. Don't bring it any further than that or you will be blunting, not sharpening, your tool.

Then, keeping the whole bevel against the wheel, swing the tool handle around in a smooth arc so that you are moving from the side, around the front to the other side of the tool. Sparks will (but not always) fly over the top of the tool (see **6**–**7**).

5–**7** Sharpening the half-round nose scraper.

8 Sharpening the half-round nose scraper.

Once you have scribed the full arc, draw the tool off the wheel (see **8**). Check the bevel and edge to see that you have touched the whole bevel and that the edge has no rough, shiny or uneven spots. Repeat the process if necessary, but aim for only one or two passes. You will be wasting good tool steel otherwise.

For the round nose scraper, my preference is to start with the tool in line with the wheel – at the centre of the sharp end. Swing the tool round so that one side of the round nose has been touched up. Then, draw the tool back off the wheel, go back to the centre and repeat the sharpening while swinging the round nose around the opposite side. Keep the movement smooth-flowing.

Parting tools

There are two sides to the parting tool, but it is not a difficult tool to sharpen. As with the scrapers, start by bringing the heel of the bevel to the wheel first (see **9**).

Next, raise the handle until the whole bevel is in contact with the wheel (see **10**). Make it a definite, firm but gentle action. Don't put too much pressure on the tool against the wheel and don't hold it there for any length of time. Work at getting a smooth movement: heel, whole bevel, off the wheel. Repeat the process for the second side, and then check the bevel and edge. With a fairly long bevel and fairly sharp angle, the concave hollow grind on the bevel should be very obvious on this tool (see **1**).

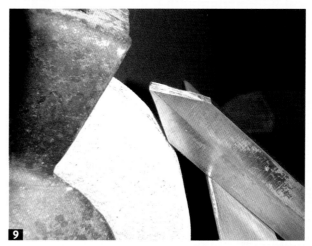

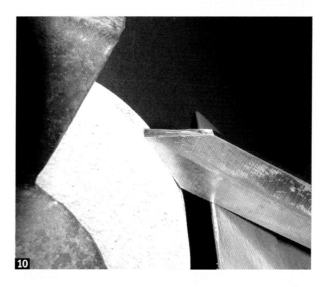

9 – **10** Sharpening the parting tool.

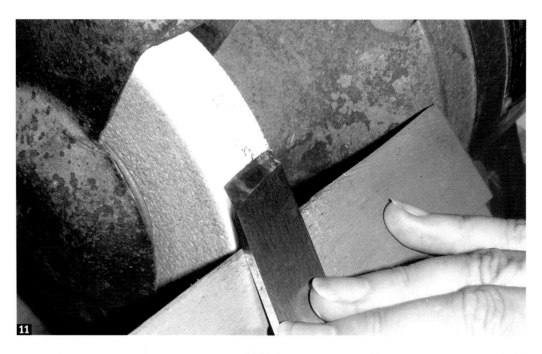

Skew chisel

The skew chisel has to be held at an angle to the wheel for sharpening in order to maintain the skewed sharp edge at the top of the tool. Bring the heel of the bevel up to the wheel first, then the whole bevel. You may need to move the tool gently backwards and forwards across the wheel to sharpen the whole width of the edge. The hardest part of sharpening the skew is maintaining the angle across the top and the bevel angle while getting a good, even grind across the whole bevel. It is very easy to end up with a lot of different facets on the bevel. This is where the table serves its purpose. It is set to maintain that bevel angle while the skew is held flat on the whole table.

Repeat the process on the other side and then check your bevels and edge for the hollow grind and for a clean, sharp edge all the way across.

11–**12** Sharpening the skew: held flat on the platform at an angle to the grinder – first one side, then the other.

Gouges

There are considerable differences of opinion about the best-shaped grind for bowl gouges. When they are bought off the shelf, they are usually ground fairly steeply and straight around at the top. My preference is to take those side wings off, as they can be dangerous in many situations.

Many turners prefer to grind even further down the sides of the flute. This gives plenty of scope for shear cutting where the tool is presented side-on to the spinning wood with the flute facing down at 7 o'clock and almost unseen by the operator. The edge of the blade on the side of the tool cuts the wood at an angle, in much the same way as a planer blade, and produces a lovely clean surface.

It is also common practice to soften the heel of the bevel, particularly at the top of the tool. This reduces the likelihood of the back edge of the bevel producing a secondary cut which shows up as a series of lines in a bowl, especially when the tool is travelling around tight curves on the inside.

For freehand grinding with the bowl gouge, start with the tool facing and in line with the wheel. Touch the heel on the wheel first and then bring the whole bevel up to contact the wheel. Keep the tool on the tool rest.

Bowl gouge showing ground profile well down the sides.

Grinding the bowl gouge: first touch the heel of the bevel on the wheel. Then raise the back of the handle until the whole of the bevel is on the wheel.

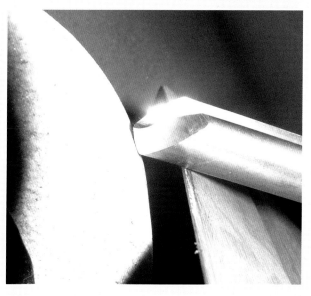

48

Grinding the gouge (continued): roll the tool around and grind down one side.

Repeat the rolling action to grind down the second side.

With the whole bevel in continuous contact with the wheel, roll the tool around and down one side. Repeat for the opposite side, then check for an even grind on the bevel and the edge.

With a roughing gouge, the process is the same, except that you do not sharpen down the sides of the tool. Beware of over-sharpening in the centre of the tool. It must remain flat across the top edge.

With a detail or spindle gouge, again, the process is the same as that for the bowl gouge, except that the bevel angle is sharper. The shape of the grind for this tool is often described as 'a lady's fingernail' because it is nice and slender and stylish, coming almost to a point in the centre at the top.

Detail gouges with the lady's fingernail grind.

6

The Wood

50

Sourcing wood

One common question I get is, 'Where do you get your wood?' My answer is, 'Everywhere and anywhere.' Not a very satisfactory answer for someone who wants specifics, but still true. I do buy wood from suppliers, but it is terribly expensive. Sometimes, I will be driving along and see someone cutting down a tree. The brakes go on, the car stops and I go and have a chat to them. I have acquired some of my nicest timbers and some good friends that way. I also have been known to acquaint myself with local tree lopping businesses and joinery workshops. I have a regular arrangement with one workshop where I buy their offcuts. I wanted it that way as, if it was to be a regular thing, I wanted to be seen as a customer rather than a freeloader. Now I am known as a local wood collector, I often get

people phoning me to ask if I want some timber. Whether I accept their offer depends on the type of wood, how long since it was cut; whether it has been lying on the ground for long; how big the pieces are and how easy it is to get the car to it. When you first start collecting, you tend to gather everything you can. Later, as the shed, under the house, the yard or any other area that promises to be a storage receptacle becomes cluttered, you start to become a little more choosy.

Green and dry wood

When wood is first cut, well over 30 per cent of its weight is water. Over time, this water is slowly lost until the wood stabilizes at around 10 per cent moisture content. Even then, wood, being an organic material, responds to atmospheric conditions by absorbing and losing moisture according to the humidity in the air.

As a general rule, moisture is lost at approximately 1in (25mm) thickness per year. However, this moisture is not being lost evenly throughout the plank or log. It is lost from the outside first – especially from the exposed ends of logs or planks. This drying wood shrinks faster than the less exposed wood, tensions are created and checks (or cracks), splits and warps occur. Therefore, if cracking is to be avoided, the wood must be processed as soon after it has been cut as possible. This involves either rough turning it, sealing the ends and/or slicing it.

> **Tip**
>
> **Goodwill goes a long way. With each gift of wood, a finished piece – usually a small bowl – is returned to the giver.**

Split ends. This wood is really only good for very small items. It will take a lot of cutting to get good bits from it.

Green wood can be used for some turning, particularly bowls and hollow vessels, provided the walls of the turned bowl or vessel are kept an even thickness throughout. A bowl can be rough turned to a thickness of about 1in (25mm), then stored for six to twelve months in a cool, still, dry place where air can circulate freely. Turned and stored like this, the wood might warp, but shouldn't crack. If it does, it will usually be in areas of end grain or around a knot or pith.

Other alternative storage methods to speed up the drying process include storing rough-turned work in the freezer and later the refrigerator; or immersing the work in drums of water for three to six weeks and then air drying for another two weeks before finishing.

After the roughed-out bowl has dried, it is re-turned on the lathe and finished. Alternatively, a bowl can be turned thinly and finished in one session. If this is done, the best finish to use is

oil – a number of successive coats over a few days. The oil tends to soak into the wood and replace moisture as it is lost.

It is not advisable to use green wood for spindle work, such as furniture legs, candlesticks and goblets; particularly where there is detailed decoration such as beads, coves and protruding pieces. These pieces would dry out and crack very quickly. Similarly, dry timber must be used for lidded boxes and any piece where different components fit together or are glued together. In these types of turning, any further moisture loss and consequent movement of the wood would destroy the fit of the lid or cause glued components to come apart.

If freshly cut timber is not to be turned immediately, at least the end grain of logs should be coated with a sealant. Commercial end-grain sealants are available; paint, paraffin wax or a mixture of PVA glue and water can also be used. Bark on the logs should be removed to prevent the likelihood of insect infestations, even though the wood is directly exposed to the air. The logs should then be stored in a cool, dry place, off the ground, with still air to allow the drying process to proceed at a slow and hopefully more even pace.

The wood has been slabbed and cut to usable sizes. The larger slabs have been end-coated to reduce moisture loss and cracking. The date of storage has been marked on some of them and the sticks placed between them allow airflow.

The outdoor rack keeps green wood off the ground and there is plenty of air, although there is perhaps still too much exposure to the elements. The roof overhang could have been greater. The undercover and under-bench stores are for dry wood. Use of the space underneath the racks risks an insect invasion. It really should be left clear.

If the full-sized log is not needed, splitting is also reduced if it is rip-sawn down the length of the log, so that it is cut into at least two sides or a number of slabs. One of the cuts should be through the central pith of the log. A large bandsaw or a chainsaw fitted with a rip saw chain is needed for this. Alternatively, if you have a number of large logs to process, it might be worthwhile calling in a professional portable saw miller.

Reducing the thickness of the wood speeds up the drying time and makes the drying more even through the whole of the split slabs or planks. Once the wood is cut, it also needs to be stored off the ground and out of the weather and stacked so that there is air circulating freely between the slabs. To ensure this, it is common practice for narrow, square, scrap lengths of wood or 'sticks' to be placed at regular intervals between slabs, as they are stacked.

The best woods for turning

An answer to this will depend firstly on timbers that are available in the local area, and secondly, on what you want to turn. For example, a very hard, dense timber might be an excellent choice for fine spindle turning of chess pieces, but would be hard going if hollowing work were to be attempted.

As a general rule, the best, or easiest wood for turning is one that is a medium density, relatively close-grained timber. Most of the fruit woods tend to fall into this close-grained category,

although there is a tendency for some of them to split. Very hard timbers usually give you a lovely finish, but you can only take small shavings and you have to sharpen the tools more frequently. Very soft, lightweight timbers are difficult to get a clean finish on. Also, unless you are going to colour it, burn it, cover it in resin or adulterate in some other way, look for an attractive timber.

The table below lists, continent by continent, some of the best turning timbers. However, it is by no means exhaustive.

Suitable turning timbers

Africa	Padauk, bubinga, ebony, zebrano, pink ivory, imbuia, jacaranda, red pear, wild olive, bushveldt resin tree, kiaat
Asia	Satinwood, Indian rosewood, ebony, ramu, teak, New Guinea rosewood
Australia	Camphor laurel, silky oak, blackwood, blackheart sassafras, myrtle, huon pine, jarrah, lace she oak, black bean (very toxic), gidgee, lancewood, rosewood, mulga, brigalow
Europe	Plane, lime, elm, boxwood, chestnut, ash, walnut
New Zealand & Pacific Islands	Rimu, kwila, matai, rata, maire, kauri, kahikatea, puriri, rewarewa, taraire, Norfolk Island pine
North America	Maple, red alder, birch, beech, ash, cherry, basswood, walnut, osage orange, mesquite, box elder, buckeye, olive woods, carob, black acacia, hackberry
South America	Parana pine, brazilwood, goncalo alves (tiger wood), kingwood, cocobolo, lignum vitae, ironwood, mahogany

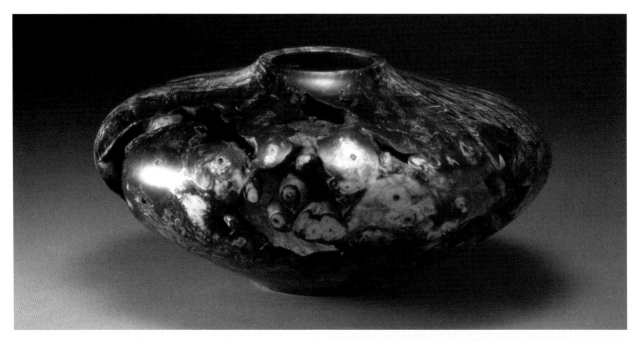

'Approaching Darkness'. Buckeye burl hollow form; 9½in diameter x 4¾in tall (241 x 120mm).

Imperfections such as wild grain, bark inclusions, prominent annual rings and rot make it difficult to obtain an even cut and a smooth finish, and the beginner turner is advised to avoid them. However, it is often these very 'imperfections' that give interest to a finished turned piece. Burls (or burrs) with random grain, bark inclusions and often areas of weakness, are much treasured by experienced turners for the beautiful bowls, vessels and sculptures that can be turned from them.

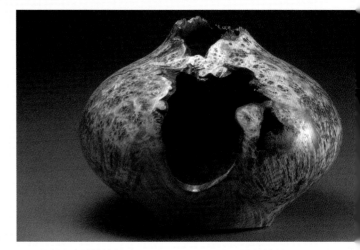

'Two Step'. Cottonwood burl hollow vessel; 11½in diameter x 9in tall (292 x 228mm). Maloof oil finish.

Identifying timbers

Identifying a piece of wood that you have come across or that someone has given you is a fairly common problem experienced by wood turners. There are a number of ways to approach the problem – each may or may not give you the satisfactory answer you want in a specific situation.

Firstly, books describing timbers might give you some idea as to what your piece of wood might be. However, in most cases, you are likely to come away from the books with two or three possibilities and no real certainty as to what it is. Books are most useful if you have some idea, and you simply want to check it out. They also help give you knowledge of a range of timbers that might be available in a particular locality.

Sometimes, satisfaction in the form of getting a definite identification doesn't come easily. The secret is patience and perseverance. Over time, as you keep asking and researching, your own knowledge base will broaden and you too will be able to help others identify their own pieces of wood.

The best chance you might have of identifying that bit of wood is to find someone who is familiar with it. Such a person might be another wood turner. Alternatively, there are clubs throughout the world of people whose hobby is to collect samples of, and identify, timbers. You often find these groups at wood shows and, usually, these people are only too happy to share their knowledge with you. Another avenue is to find a timber specialist in the local government forestry department, or even a local timber dealer or saw miller.

Toxic woods

All wood dust is toxic. Our lungs and respiratory system do have the ability to self-cleanse under normal conditions. However, if we are standing and turning for a number of hours at a time or for a number of days at a time, we are overloading our system with dust and, over time, it will affect us, even if we are only turning the 'safe' timbers. We can experience shortness of breath, asthma symptoms, nosebleeds, skin irritation and rashes, dizziness and a multitude of other unpleasant symptoms, and there is also the potential for cancer.

Of course, some timbers are worse than others. It isn't possible in this book to give a comprehensive list of all of them. It does pay to do a bit of research of your own before you start turning a new timber. If the timber is locally grown, ask other turners and woodworkers about their experiences with it. If you know the name of the timber, do some research. There are a number of good websites (at the time of writing, www.ubeaut.com.au/badwood.htm is a good one), which list timbers and their known effects. You could also contact your local government forestry department and see if they can provide you with any information. Finally, if you don't know the name of the timber, or can't find any satisfactory or conclusive information about its toxicity, then treat it as if it were toxic.

To play safe, use a good mask all the time, or better still, a full helmet respirator. Also, cover up your skin and wear a good barrier cream on your hands, especially in hot weather. The pores in your skin can absorb toxic dust and are also vulnerable. To be even safer, avoid the known 'baddies' altogether. The risk to your health isn't worth it.

Stabilizing wood

Wood that has cracks, wild grain that tends to chip out and areas where there are bark inclusions all make the turning of these pieces rather hazardous. However, it is often these 'flaws' in the wood that make the finished turning interesting. So, we take the risk and there are few turners who do not have at least one story of the piece that exploded on the lathe and went flying across the room. Some have the scars to prove it.

For small 'flaws', superglue (cyanoacrylate) is the most commonly used stabilizer. Used with a spray-on accelerator it dries almost instantly.

56

To fill cracks, wood dust can be pressed into the crack first, then superglue and accelerator applied. I have found though, that if you re-apply more superglue and accelerator, it often goes white. Superglue is also useful for hardening and attaching bark inclusions and stabilizing areas of torn end grain when a good, sanded finish is difficult to obtain.

White PVA glue can also be used to fill cracks. Save some of the dust from the bandsaw or from sanding on the lathe, mix it with the glue, press it in and wipe off the excess with a damp cloth. Give the glue time to set before switching on the lathe or you may be wearing the glue and dust mix on your face.

If you are hollowing a piece that is a bit suspect (such as one with a hole in one side or a crack that might open up, or even some laminated pieces that might fly off), it can be held together by masking tape, plastic wrap or hose clamps while the hollowing is in progress. It is also wise to slow the lathe down a bit more than normal while turning these pieces. If the weakness is very obvious or the piece is flimsy once the finishing is being done, a bit of decorative binding with leather thongs, iron nails, barbed wire or any other interesting material could be employed to strengthen the piece and to add character.

There are also epoxy-based materials on the market, which are specifically designed as timber primers and sealers. They come as a two-pack and, when thinned down, can be used as a wood saturation system to help harden, densify and seal out moisture in the timber.

Casting resin, which is also a two-pack resin and hardener, can also be used decoratively to fill and stabilize weaknesses and holes. It comes clear, but a whole range of colours, opaque and translucent, can be mixed in with the resin. Solid bits – seed pods, nut shells, glitter, dried flowers, chips of semi-precious stone, insects, and so on – can also be embedded into the resin or directly into the wood as part of your work of art.

Stabilizing grub dust with superglue (cyanoacrylate). The spots usually remain darker, but look better than a hole in the wrong place.

If you do plan to use resin, make sure you read and comply with all the safety instructions accompanying the resin. It and its fumes are toxic. Also, once the resin and the hardener are mixed, you usually have around ten to thirty minutes to use it before it gels.

Heat is a problem when using casting resin. Once the resin and hardener are mixed, the chemical reaction generates heat. This causes the resin to expand. Once the reaction slows down, the resin then contracts and pulls away from the edges leaving an untidy gap. To deal with this, the reaction time needs to be slowed down by adding less hardener or by pouring small successive layers of resin until the hole is filled. Each new layer is poured once the previous layer becomes tacky.

Dogwood knot bowl with walnut shell insert.

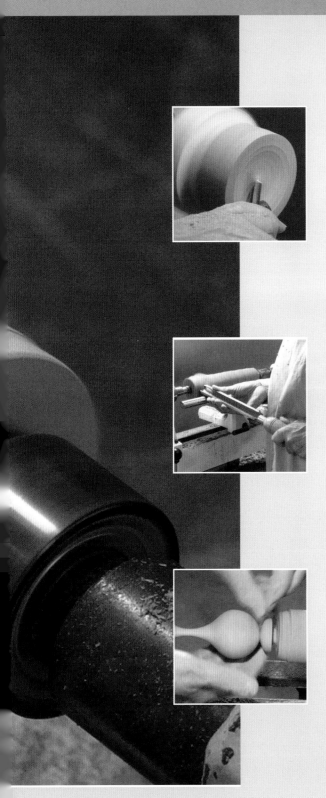

Basic Turning and Tools

7

Starting Turning

Learning woodturning

Starting out can be an exciting, but sometimes daunting process. You might find yourself in front of the lathe with tool and block of wood in hand, with the question, 'What do I do now?' Confident individuals blaze away, try what seems to be the right way, make some mistakes and develop some bad habits, but generally succeed in producing something and making some progress. Books on woodturning are a great help and I remember often standing in front of the lathe, with tool in one hand and book in the other, working out what to do and how to do it.

If there's a woodworkers' club in the local area, it would pay to visit them a couple of times and possibly join up. There are usually people in the clubs who you can ask for help and advice. Go to demonstrations and ask plenty of questions and then try out what you have seen demonstrated. Finally, if there is a woodturning instructor with a good reputation, get some

lessons (but not all good woodturners make good instructors). With proper instruction, encouragement and practice, you will make rapid progress. Keep the bevel rubbing and play!

Getting the centre

If you are going to turn square stock between centres (spindle work), you can get the centre of each end by placing a ruler or straight edge on the diagonals and pencilling in a crisscross. Where the lines meet will be the centre.

If you are going to be mounting a number of same-size spindle blanks on the lathe, it might pay to make up a centre punch box. Cut a square block of wood from a plank. Make it the width of the stock you wish to mark plus the width of the wood making up the walls of the box. Slightly wider is better than slightly narrower. It should mount in your four-jaw chuck. If not, use hot melt glue to glue it onto a scrap disc that will fit into the chuck. On the face of the block, turn down a circle that is the same diameter (or marginally larger) as the width of the stock on which you wish to mark centres. The circle need only be ³/₁₆in (5mm) deep. The sides of the circle must be perfectly straight. Using a small drill bit in a Jacob's chuck, drill a hole right through the centre of it. Remove the block from the lathe and hammer a short nail (fatter than the hole you drilled so that it stays put) from the back through the drilled centre hole. It should protrude about ³/₁₆in (5mm) above the circle. Then construct the box – glue and screw or glue and nail – to fit flush around the circle.

Crossing the diagonals on end grain stock to get the centre.

◤ A home-made centre find box for marking the ends of spindle blanks.

Once the box is completed, push the square stock into it. If it is a slightly sloppy fit, twist the stock until its edges touch the box walls. Push down hard so that the point of the nail marks the end of the wood. That should be your centre. If you are marking lots of stock the same size, this does save a lot of time.

If the piece you wish to mount is not square or is a log, the quickest way to guess the centre is to mount it between centres and spin it by hand. You will soon see which side is the heaviest and you can adjust your mounting accordingly.

A centre find – a plastic device with 60° and 90° raised angles – is also useful for finding the centre on square, round and hexagonal stock. You sit the find over the piece, mark along the central straight line, rotate it to about 90° and mark again.

If the circle of wood is too large for the centre find and very rough, you can use a series of cardboard discs which have been scribed with a compass, leaving the centre point marked, then cut out. A disc that is slightly smaller than the wood is placed over it and moved around until it makes the best fit. The centre hole is then marked by pressing in a drawing pin, or marking through with a felt pen. These cardboard discs are also useful as templates for cutting out blanks on the bandsaw.

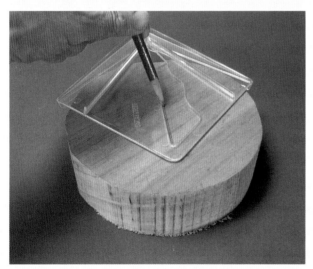

Using a centre find guide.

◤ Cardboard discs are useful as templates for cutting discs and finding centres on rough stock.

Mounting spindle work between centres

Once you have got the centre on your spindle blank, it can be mounted between the drive centre in the headstock and the live tailstock centre. With hard wood, it is a good idea to use a mallet to hit the drive centre into the centre point of the wood while it is off the lathe. Make sure the sharp drive dogs on either side of the centre point dig in, then mount the whole thing on the lathe. That way, you aren't putting pressure on the lathe bearings when you bring up the tailstock and tighten it up. With softer woods, I usually just mount the piece straight into the lathe. Don't forget to lock the tailstock off once you have wound it in enough.

Once the log or square stock is mounted securely between centres on the lathe, lock in the tool rest so that the top of the rest is a tool thickness below centre height and as close as is safely possible to the blank without the blank touching it. Spin the blank by hand to see that it doesn't hit the tool rest.

The height of the rest is crucial for comfortable turning. Once you start work, you will feel whether the tool rest is too high or too low. If, as you progress, a sharp tool is not cutting well or if you are having to hold it at an uncomfortable level, stop the lathe and adjust the tool rest up or down. As a general rule, the tool's edge should be cutting at centre height. You will eventually get the feel of what the right height should be.

▶ The piece mounted between the headstock drive centre and the live tailstock centre. The tool rest should be as close as is safely possible to the work and a bit below centre height. Spin the work by hand before switching on the lathe to see that it is clear of the tool rest.

Using a mallet to embed the drive centre before mounting the work between centres.

Lock off the tailstock to finish mounting the piece securely.

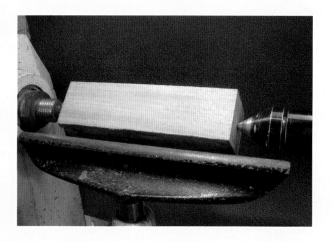

◀ A range of four-jaw expanding chucks with some of the different jaws available. Top left: Nova chuck with standard jaws; beneath it are screw chuck with home-made washer, C and straight bar for adjusting the jaw opening, shark jaws and Allen key. Top centre: VM 90 chuck fitted with long nose jaws; beneath it are pin jaws, inserts to fit different screw threads on lathes and bars for adjusting jaw width. Top right: VM 120 chuck with standard jaws; beneath it are wide dovetail jaws, bars and shark jaws.

Mounting work in a chuck

The most commonly used chucks today are the four-jaw expanding chucks, which can be used in expansion and contraction mode. They make holding work on the lathe quick and easy. They have virtually replaced cup chucks, which were basically slightly tapered cylinders into which the stock was belted with a mallet. Some old turners used to bash the stock straight into the headstock. It must have been hard on the lathe drive bearings. For spindle or end grain work, the chuck comes into its own when it is necessary for the tailstock end to be left free: for drilling, hollowing or simply for sanding the end of a piece; and for pieces using inserts, such as clocks, goblets, lidded boxes, vases, handles and spinning tops.

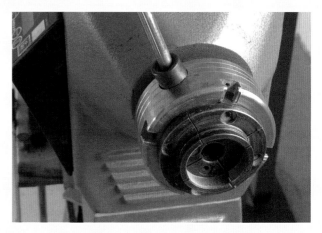

The supernova chuck with T-bar tightening system. Tightening of the chuck jaws can be done one-handed, leaving the other hand free to hold the wood steady. One chuck with standard jaws is quite adequate for the beginner just setting up.

1–**4** Using the chuck when the end of a piece of spindle work has to be operated on – when drilling, hollowing or simply neat finishing. In **3**, the spinning top is first held in a chuck as well as being supported by the tailstock while being shaped. One of the final cuts is with the skew to remove the scrappy piece at the tailstock and form a nice point. The spinning top will then be sanded, supported only from the chuck on the headstock. Small section blocks can be mounted straight in the chuck as in **1** and **4**. Wider pieces must be mounted between centres and then a spigot turned (see **5**) to enable mounting in the chuck. This is the case with the pot in **2**.

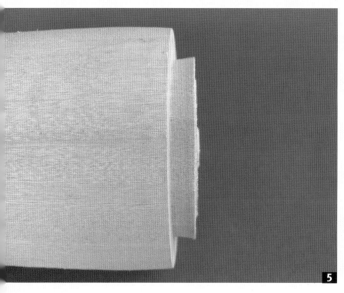

◀ Wide pieces are first mounted between centres and roughed down to a cylinder. A spigot, which is wider on the outside end than further in, is turned on the end of the cylinder. This spigot fits into and is gripped by the chuck jaws.

The screw chuck and home-made shims for when the piece to be mounted is fairly shallow.

The screw chuck mounted in the four-jaw chuck. The end shoulder of the screw chuck must sit flush with the back of the jaws for the screw chuck to run true.

Drilling the screw hole. The drill bit must be a slightly smaller diameter than the screw chuck to leave some timber for the screw threads to grip onto.

Using a screw chuck

The screw chuck usually comes as part of the four-jaw chuck. It can be used instead of a faceplate to mount small cross-grain work such as wine bottle coasters, bottle openers and small bowls.

Friction chucking

For small cross-grain pieces, you can mount a blank on the lathe by simply marking its centre and bringing up the tailstock to press the blank between the open chuck and the tailstock point. Tailstock centres with a cup and point are best for this. It is the point in the wood, and friction, which hold the blank on the lathe. Reduce the speed a bit and cut a dovetail-shaped spigot. The piece can then be reversed and held in contraction mode in the four-jaw chuck.

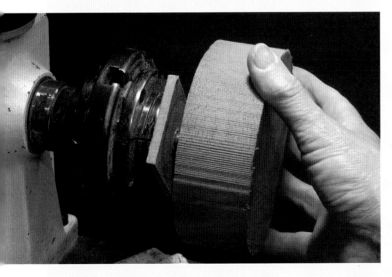

◀ Mounting the piece. Hold the wood steady and turn the headstock by hand until the block is screwed in to sit flush against the top of the chuck jaws or the shim if one is fitted on the screw chuck.

Faceplate mounting: the start of a natural edge bowl. The bark and the natural shape of the log is retained in the rim of the bowl. The centre of the blank is established and a small faceplate screwed on. An area in the centre has been slightly carved away so the faceplate can sit flat.

The outside of the bowl turned and sanded. For turning the inside, this bowl will be gripped in expansion mode – hence the dovetailed recess in the foot.

Faceplate mounting

The faceplate has been the traditional form of mounting for cross-grain work, especially bowls. In the past, before chucks were in common use, the faceplate was screwed to the bottom of the bowl blank with relatively short screws and the outside and inside of the bowl turned on the one mounting. The disadvantages were that the width of the bowl's foot was limited to the width of the faceplate or wider; and that the screw marks had to be somehow concealed once the bowl was removed from the faceplate. Most turners either filled the holes with putty or glued a piece of felt on the base. This covered up a multitude of sins. Now it is common practice to screw the faceplate onto what will be the top of the bowl, turn, sand and finish the base and the outside of the bowl, leaving a spigot, a recess or a foot to be gripped in the chuck. Once the faceplate is removed and the bowl reversed and gripped by the chuck, the inside is hollowed out. If a recess has been turned in the base, the chuck can be used in expansion mode to hold the bowl. Any marks will not be seen once the work comes off the lathe.

This bowl was gripped on the foot in contraction mode while the inside was being hollowed. It was then reversed on the lathe to clean up the marks left on the foot by the chuck jaws. The shoulder or bead between foot and bowl hides any imperfections that might come about if the reversed bowl can't be centred perfectly. The central mark on the underside of the foot shows where the tailstock point was brought up to hold the bowl against a padded disc on the lathe. This can later be sanded out.

Holding stock without a four-jaw chuck

However, if the turner wishes to enter the bowl in a competition, there should be no evidence of how the work was held. The chuck can also be used in contraction mode to grip a spigot or foot on the base of the bowl. Once the inside has been hollowed and finished, the bowl has to be reversed and re-chucked, usually by friction or in a jam-fit chuck to remove the spigot or marks made by the chuck on the foot.

Using faceplates, jam-fit chucks and glue are just some of the different methods of mounting work on the lathe and this has been one area where woodturners have shown great ingenuity. While the four-jaw chuck makes mounting very easy and will be the preferred method many times over, there are more ways than one to 'skin a cat' or, in this case, hold some work on the lathe.

If a turner wishes to hollow a lidded box, end-grain work has to be mounted so the tailstock end is free. Without a four-jaw chuck, he or she can go back to some of the older, tried-and-tested methods. These include using the hollow in the headstock to hold the work; or using the faceplate, in conjunction with a glued waste block and/or a jam-fit chuck.

Using the headstock hollow

The first way is to mount your stock between centres, rough it down to a cylinder and then turn a spigot approximately 1in (25mm) long. The spigot must be the diameter of the hollow in the headstock, or slightly wider, and tapered a bit at the end. This spigot is then bashed into the headstock with a mallet so that it is nice and firm. Bring the tailstock up to give a bit of extra support while you are shaping the outside and the lid, and remove it when you need to do the hollowing of the box. Once you have turned your box (without getting a catch) and parted it off, there is a stub left in the headstock. Knock it out from the other end of the headstock with a knockout bar. This is a method used by the old-time production turners long before four-jaw chucks were developed. It was very quick and they used to make all sorts of small items that needed to be free of the tailstock point at some time in the turning, such as light pulls, tops and shaving brushes. It must have been tough on the lathe bearings, though, and would really only be safe for small things.

Gluing to a waste block

The second method of holding work involves using the faceplate (preferably a small one), a scrap block and some PVA wood glue.

You simply glue the end of the block to be used for the box to the scrap block and then screw that to the faceplate. Since you are gluing at least one bit of end grain, make sure it is well coated with glue and that the glue is dry before you start turning. Stick to wide, and relatively low boxes using this method just to be on the safe side. Also, bring the tailstock up for that extra support whenever you aren't hollowing.

Making a jam-fit chuck

The third method of holding your lidded box will also give you a home-made chuck, which you can use to make any number of lidded boxes. Mount the wood that is to become the lidded box between centres, rough it down to a cylinder and face off the cylinder at both ends. Aim to have both ends of the cylinder the same diameter. Part the cylinder through about two-thirds up. The smaller piece will then be used for the lid.

Screw a scrap wooden disc at least ¾in (19mm) thick (preferably more) onto a faceplate. Try to keep the screws away from the centre of the disc. This is your wooden faceplate that the work will be glued to – first the lid, then later, the box base.

Tip

Even if you do possess a four-jaw chuck, wooden jam-fit chucks are very handy for reversing lidded boxes and bowls to clean up the base of the work. Unlike the four-jaw chuck, the wooden jam-fit chuck leaves no mark when the finished piece is taken off the lathe. Simply save your scrap blocks to make these chucks when they are needed.

Making and using a jam-fit chuck:
1 screw a waste block onto a faceplate.
2 Measure the diameter of the cylinder that will be the lid to the box.
3 – **4** Transfer that diameter onto the spinning block with dividers or vernier callipers. Only touch the spinning wood with one of the points and use the other as a guide.

True up the face of it on the lathe, and then use a Jacob's chuck to drill a hole right through the centre of the wooden faceplate. Use a fairly large drill bit, about ⅜in (9.5mm). The hole allows air to escape later when you will jam the cylinder in and also gives you a start when cutting a recess. Measure the diameter of your cylinder and mark that diameter on the faceplate. You can do that with a ruler, but better still, use dividers or vernier callipers if you have them.

Starting from the central drill hole, use a square nose scraper to cut the recess about ⅜in (9.5mm) deep with a diameter the same as the cylinder. Take care not to make the diameter too wide. You want to jam (hence the name jam-chuck) your spigot into the recess. When you get close to the right diameter, take very fine cuts and test fit after each cut.

Next, you can glue your cylinder into the recess using PVA wood glue or hot melt glue. PVA wood glue makes it more solid, but will take

Test to see if the cylinder fits.

The cylinder is jammed into the wooden chuck.

72

Using hot melt glue or masking tape to make the jam-fit more secure. You can also bring the tailstock up for extra support until you need to hollow out the centre.

time to cure and you will have to turn the waste out later if you wish to use the faceplate chuck again. Alternatively, if hot melt glue is used to hold the cylinder into the recess, turning can start within a couple of minutes of gluing. Also, the waste can be prised out of the recess once you have parted off your box and the faceplate chuck can be used again. First, chisel out a groove away from one side of the recess, about the width of a knife. This groove is so you can later get a knife in to prise the waste out. Hot melt glue has good holding power, but is weak when leverage is applied. Alternatively, wrap masking tape around the join and bring the

Turning a lidded box using a jam-fit chuck: **1** start by turning and finishing the inside of the lid; **2** shape and finish the bottom of the outside, then part or lever that out. Next, fit the base and hot melt glue or tape it in. Continue as if you were turning a box with a standard chuck: turn a spigot on the top of the base to fit the lid; fit the lid on and bring up the tailstock; shape the outside and finish the lid; then remove the lid and hollow and finish the inside of the base. Part off the base and clean up the bottom using a power sanding attachment gripped in either the lathe or the drill press (see chapter 8, project 2, pages 93–102).

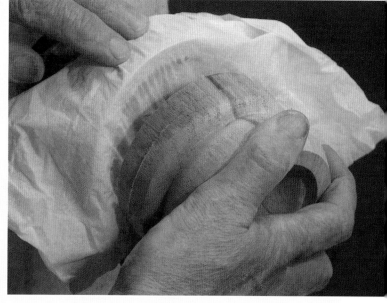

If the recess you have cut in the wooden chuck is a tiny bit big, you can swell the wood slightly by painting the recess wall and the cylinder with water, or put a layer of tissue in the chuck, and then jam the cylinder in. It works, but a bit of hot melt glue or masking tape should also help.

How important is grain direction?

Think of wood as a whole lot of fibres laid down parallel to each other and stuck together. These fibres run the full length of the tree trunk and the branches. The longer those fibres are in a piece of turning, the more chance they have of sticking to other fibres around them and therefore the stronger the wood in the turned piece. So, if you are going to turn a table leg or a tall candle holder (a long, thin piece of wood), you will want to have the grain parallel to the lathe bed and turn between centres (spindle work). Alternatively, if you wish to turn a large, shallow platter, you need to have the grain running across the diameter of the platter for it to have any strength. You will be turning 'cross grain'. For a deep bowl, you could either turn cross grain (with the grain at 90° to the lathe bed), as with the platter, or end grain, with the grain or fibres parallel to the lathe bed.

Lathe speeds

Although I have seen books that contain tables giving the relationship between the size of a piece of wood and the speed at which it should be spun on a lathe, there really aren't any hard-and-fast rules about what speed you should be operating at. As a general rule, the larger and more out of balance a piece of wood, the slower the speed should be. However, the faster the wood is spinning, the easier it is to get a clean cut with the tools. You are playing a balancing act between safety and ease of turning.

A small piece of spindle work, such as a pen or a wine bottle cork or small finial, can be spun somewhere between 2,000 to 3,000 rpm, whereas a large log has to be spun down around 500 rpm, or lower. For a bowl with a 9in (228mm) diameter, start around 1,200 rpm. Then, when some of the bulk has been removed and if it feels a bit slow, increase the speed a bit. You could also bring the tailstock up for a bit of extra security while you are roughing the blank out.

The deciding factor is safety. If the lathe vibrates madly and starts to edge its way across the floor or the piece looks and sounds like it is going to become airborne, then obviously, the speed is too fast. You can always start a piece slowly and then increase the speed once it is roughed out.

When you reach sanding time, slow the lathe down. You have many small bits of grit on the sandpaper connecting with the spinning wood and heat is generated quickly. This heat can cause small checks or cracks to appear, especially in end grain. Once they are there, you won't be able to sand them out.

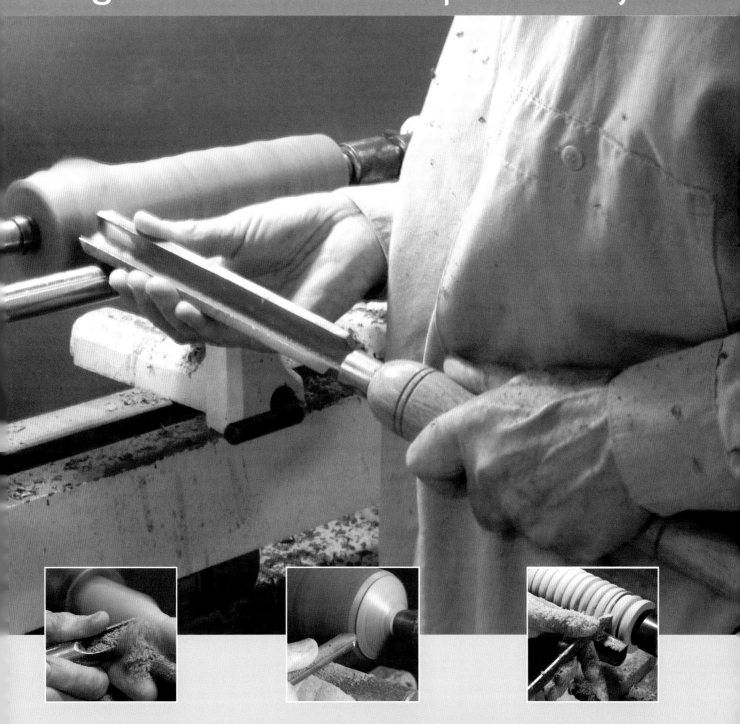

8

Using the Tools – Techniques & Projects

76

This chapter is designed to give the beginner and intermediate turner some techniques and projects for developing skills in using each of the main tools. The projects covered have been selected because they employ a wide range of tools and holding techniques. Most of them are ones I use with my woodturning students. There are some elements of repetition between the techniques and projects sections. This is deliberate – think of it as reinforcing. It is recommended that you read the techniques section a couple of times, to get an idea of how to use the tools (maybe even with tool in hand so that you can go through the motions), then try the projects. If you are unfamiliar with any of the terms used in this section, refer to the glossary on pages 184–187.

Techniques

Roughing out spindle work

The roughing out gouge is used primarily to bring a log or square stock down to a cylinder in preparation for further shaping. The large bowl gouge, which I prefer, can also be used for this.

Start with a block of wood approximately 2in (50mm) in diameter and 4½in (114mm) long. Mount your block between centres and lock the tailstock off. Bring the tool rest up so that it is just below centre height and as close as is safely possible to the work. Spin it by hand to make sure wood and tool rest do not connect (see also chapter 7, 'Starting Turning'). Check to see that you have the lathe set at a safe speed. For a block this size, it should be set somewhere between 1,700 to 2,100 rpm.

1 I am taking successive cuts towards the tailstock, starting each cut a little further back. You can rough out this way, or you can move the gouge backwards and forwards across the whole length of the work, using your body to move the tool. Whatever takes your fancy! Just keep the handle tucked in against your side.

Turn the lathe on and stand facing the wood with your feet apart. The back end of the tool handle (provided it is a reasonably long one) should be tucked against or below your hip. Notice the angle at which the tool is held. If the back of the handle is any higher than this when the tool cuts at centre height, stop the lathe and adjust the tool rest down.

Keeping the handle close against your body, rest the tool on the tool rest, then advance it towards the spinning wood. Once you connect with the wood, do not push in any further. The first cuts should be fairly light to get the edges off. With the tool still firmly tucked against your body, use your body to move the tool across the wood. This is why your feet are apart. You can sometimes get up a good swaying action.

Once the edges are taken off, the bevel (the ground part of the tool behind the sharp edge) should be rubbing against the wood. The gouge is supported securely in three places – against your body, on the tool rest and with the bevel on the wood. In **1**, the heel of my left hand is on the tool rest and my fingers are gripping over the top of the gouge.

Continue roughing out until you get the stock down to a round cylinder. By this stage, the bevel should be rubbing against the wood. This helps support the tool on the wood and enables you to get a clean cut. As you remove waste, you may need to move the tool rest in closer to the wood. You can stop the lathe occasionally and check to see whether the stock is down to round, or you can use touch with the wood still spinning. However, do not touch the tips of your fingers onto wood spinning down towards them. You could jam them between the spinning wood and the tool rest and do some serious damage.

Once the tailstock end is roughed out, you can change hands and work towards the headstock. Learning to use both hands can be a great advantage. An alternative method of holding the tool at the tool rest is shown in 2 – with your fingers underneath and thumb on top. The index finger against the tool rest keeps the gouge steady. Use whichever method of holding is comfortable for you. A common mistake made by beginners holding the tool this way is to lift the tool right off the tool rest, relying only on that index finger for support. The result is a very sore finger once the tool cracks down hard. The tool has to stay on the rest.

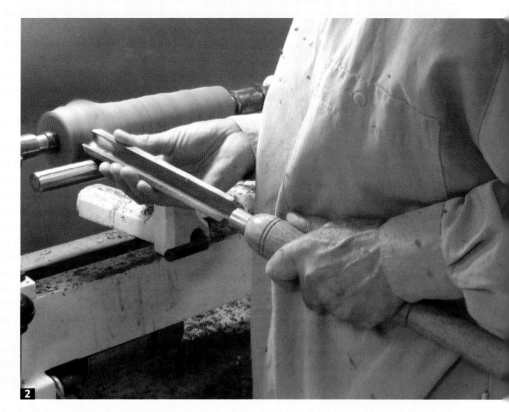

78

Touch the top of the wood behind the first joints of the fingers with the fingers together and held flat. Alternatively, put your hand above the wood and let it brush down off the tip of your thumb. You will feel any rough spots immediately.

As you get closer to achieving round stock, check yourself to see that you are still rubbing the bevel against the spinning wood. If you are, you should be getting a clean, smooth cut. If not, there are more likely to be rough and high and low points on your work where the tool has not been supported fully. At this stage, you will be ready to switch to other tools to shape the wood.

Testing for round the *wrong* way! You will do some serious damage to your fingers.

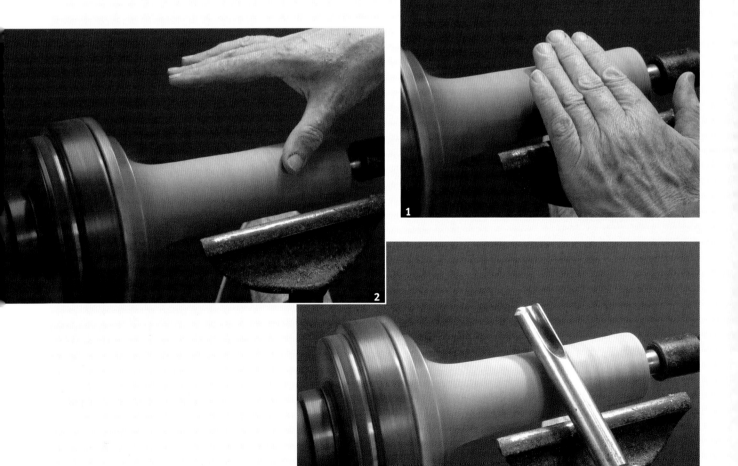

1–**3** Testing for round the safe ways.

Using a large bowl gouge

Similar techniques to those just described for the roughing gouge are employed when you use the large bowl gouge, whether you are roughing out spindle work or blanks mounted for faceplate turning of a bowl or platter.

Keep your feet wide apart, tuck the tool handle close to your body, and make sure the tool is on the tool rest before you touch it to wood. Touch the heel of the bevel on the wood first, then raise the handle until you feel the cut. The bevel should still be rubbing. Keep the tool firm, but don't push too hard into the wood or it will chatter and bounce. Keeping the tool handle tucked against your body, use your body to move the tool along or around the wood. It's almost a swaying motion.

Using a bowl gouge

The ⅜in (9.5mm) bowl gouge is perhaps the most versatile tool in the turner's toolkit. At a pinch, it can be used for roughing out. It can also be used to do a considerable amount of spindle work, some end-grain hollowing, and most faceplate work including the turning of the outside and inside of bowls. When the tool is sharp and the cut light, it is also capable of doing some fine finishing work.

Movements for cutting with the bowl gouge are similar to those used for the roughing gouge and the detail gouge. Keep your feet apart and the tool supported by your body whenever possible, and keep the bevel rubbing on the wood behind the cutting edge.

1–**2** The large bowl gouge can be used for roughing out spindle work and bowl blanks. When the bevel is rubbing, the tool is supported on the wood, producing a clean cut. **3** A bowl gouge is used to remove the bulk of the waste to shape this spinning top – first the bottom, closest to the tailstock, then the waste around the top and handle. The bevel is kept rubbing on the wood, even when the tool is cutting deep down to form the handle. The operator must be careful to avoid the sides of the flutes hitting the wood.

Establishing a bowl foot and recess. To remove waste for the recess, the cut is a shear scrape starting from the centre with the flute facing the operator, and nearly out of sight. A clean dovetail can then be cut for the recess with a skew or detail gouge. Above right, the shape under the foot is concave rather than flat. The cut starts at the edge of the foot with the flute facing away from the wood. As the cut progresses in, the tool is gradually twisted so that the flute finishes facing up towards 2 o'clock.

When doing bowl work, if the blank is unbalanced when first mounted, you may wish to bring the tailstock up for further support until it is brought into round. You will be turning the outside and bottom of the blank first and later reversing it to be gripped by a four-jaw expanding chuck in order to hollow out the top. Start working with the large bowl gouge to remove waste from the outside and bottom edges. When most of the rough edges are taken off, you will need to cut from bottom to top of the bowl (towards the faceplate) so the grain that is being cut is supported by grain underneath it.

As you work around the base, you will want to move the tool rest to ensure that the tool is never hanging too far over it. There should never be too great a space between where the tool is supported on the rest and where it is cutting the wood.

Once the worst of the excess wood is removed and it is more balanced on the lathe, you can remove the tailstock to get at the base. Work consistently around the base from bottom to top until you have got the wood to the final shape that you want the bowl to be. On the base, you will also need to establish a spigot, recess and/or foot with which to grip the bowl when you reverse it for inside hollowing.

When the bowl gouge is ground well down the sides, the side of the tool can be used to perform finishing, or shear, cuts on the outside of the bowl. These cuts leave a beautifully tooled finish ready for sanding. The tool rest is in close to the work and low. The tool handle is also held low with the flute facing about 7 o'clock, almost unseen by the operator who is rubbing the bevel and feeling for the cut. The spinning wood is peeled off in fine, curly shavings as the angled blade cuts, in much the same way as a planer blade peels off the wood.

Hollowing the inside of the bowl. Aim for a consistently smooth curve.

Using the detail gouge to face off spindle work. The bevel is rubbing and the angle that it is facing will determine the cutting angle.

Once the outside of a bowl is finished, the bowl is reversed on the lathe and the inside hollowed, still using the bowl gouge. The cut starts with the gouge held well over the lathe bed so that the bevel is almost parallel with the bed and the flute facing away from the operator. The hand holding the back of the handle (usually the right hand) then swings an arc towards the body while gradually twisting the tool so that, as the cutting edge reaches the centre of the bowl, the flute is facing upwards. It is a nice, smooth curve that the turner is producing.

Tip

When hollowing out the inside of a bowl, try to keep each pass flowing smoothly from start to finish. Use your body as much as possible to control the tool. This way, you are more likely to avoid lumpy bits halfway down the bowl and you should end up with a reasonably even wall thickness.

Using the detail gouge

Use the detail or spindle gouge with the 'lady's fingernail' grind to do fine detail on spindle work. It may not be as robust as the bowl gouge, but the flutes are shallow and it has that nice 'sweet point' at the top of the fingernail, so it is easy to get into tight spots. Use it in a similar way to the other gouges – supported on the body, the tool rest and with the bevel on the wood. The sweet point is the part of the tool that should enter the wood first, usually with the flute facing 3 or 9 o'clock. Once a shoulder has been established for the bevel to rub on, there is no danger of the tool skidding along the work and the tool can then be twisted a little so the flute is slightly more open and you get a more vigorous cut. The direction the bevel points will govern the angle of the cut you get, so as the cut progresses, move your body to get the angle you want.

82

The detail gouge can be used to face off end-grain work in much the same way as the skew chisel is used. The sweet point starts a fine cut in $\frac{1}{32}$in (less than 1mm) of wood and the tool is pushed forwards while the bevel works to support the tool on the face being cut. As the cut progresses, it is the sharp edge just below and behind the front point, which is doing most of the cutting.

1–**3** Doing fine, detailed spindle work.

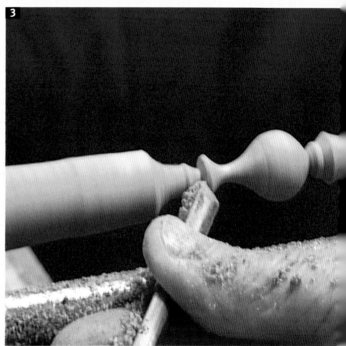

Using a skew chisel

While I have seen the skew chisel used for many purposes, including roughing out and bowl turning, it is best and most commonly used for cutting grooves, facing off end grain work, getting a clean finish on details in spindle work, and parting off fine spindle work such as finials.

The skew has three parts that can be used – the long and short points and, when turned on its side, the flat blade. I am not forgetting the bevel. This is always in use, but not for cutting.

The long point of the skew is perhaps the most useful. When using it to make a small groove in the spinning wood, simply hold the tool with the handle down low and tucked in close to your body. Move the tool in to connect with the wood and raise the back of the handle. The tip of the long point will be pushed into the wood. Pull the tool out once the cut is made to avoid burning the timber or overheating the thin steel at the point of the tool. It is a smooth and fairly quick action and you don't have to exert a great deal of pressure (see **4** on page 84). You can open out the groove to form a V cut by taking successive cuts from each side of the groove.

The action for facing off, or getting a clean end to a piece of spindle work where you are cutting through end-grain starts the same, with the tool vertical on the rest and the handle low and tucked against your body. When making the cut, all you take off is $\frac{1}{32}$in (less than 1mm) of timber. Much more than that and you will have to force the tool too much. Move the tool in to connect with the wood and gradually raise the handle as you execute the cut. Use your body to move the tool forwards into the wood. The part of the bevel just behind the point (but not further up) should be rubbing as you cut, to give the tool support on the wood. Draw the tool out once the cut is made. Projects to practise this on are foot massage rollers and spinning tops.

Often when executing facing-off cuts with the skew, kickback can occur, resulting in a nasty great spiral gash in the work. When you cut into the wood, it should only be the first $\frac{3}{64}$in (1mm) of the skew point that is cutting. The bevel just behind the cutting point should also rest on the work and you exert the force (not massive amounts) needed to produce a smooth, clean cut.

Facing off end grain with the long point of the skew chisel. Do a few small, successive cuts rather than one big one. Note the thin shaving and the clean finish on the wood.

1 – 3 Using the long point of the skew to face off top and bottom sides of a spinning top, clean up the point where handle and body connect and part off the base to produce a clean point.

Suddenly, the kickback occurs. This happens if the skew happens to twist slightly and more than $\frac{3}{64}$in (1mm) of the skew has suddenly connected with the wood. You are still exerting the same amount of force needed to push $\frac{3}{64}$in (1mm) of metal through the wood. However, it's not enough to push $\frac{3}{32}$in (2mm) or more through. The downward force of the spinning wood is greater than the force you are exerting on the tool. Something (the tool) has got to give. Hey presto, the nasty gash. It happens in a split second – faster than your brain can register that conditions at the cutting edge have changed. The secret is to keep the skew vertical. Consistently rubbing the bevel just behind the point and ensuring that you are cutting with the point only should also help.

The flat blade of the skew can be used to execute a planing cut on relatively flat spindle work or on a slightly curving surface. Done properly, on even-grained wood, it produces a very smooth, tooled finish. To do this, the tool is laid on its side on the tool rest and the bevel of the bottom third of the blade (closest to the short point) is laid on the wood. This is most easily done with the tool rest raised a bit so the tool rides along the top of the wood. Once you get the

4 Using the skew to get a clean cut when parting off work. The right hand rests on the tailstock and supports the work and the thumb helps support the tool.

hang of it, you won't need to raise the tool rest, as you will be able to feel where the tool needs to be. Gently twist the tool so the edge of the blade starts to cut and fine, curly shavings or dust start coming off. Gradually move the tool along the wood, maintaining the same height and angle.

You will feel if you aren't maintaining the correct cut. If you dig the blade into the wood too far, there will be greater resistance and you will have to force it too much. If you allow any more than the bottom third of the blade to cut, you will get a dig-in.

The long or short points, along with $\frac{3}{64}$–$\frac{3}{32}$in (1–2mm) of the blade behind them, can also be used in the planing cut mode to lift up and curl surface grain. Adjust your angle so that the point and not the flat of the blade is connecting the wood, and twist it slightly more so that it digs in slightly. This technique is useful if you want to create a Christmas tree effect on a cone-shaped piece of wood, or if you make a mushroom and want to create the impression of gills on the underside of the mushroom hat.

Finally, we come to the short point of the skew. Some turners feel safer using the short rather than the long point, but I tend not to use it for facing off or cutting into spindle work, simply because it isn't so easy to see what the point is doing.

The rest of the tool is in the way. However, when I wish to cut a very deep, narrow round-bottom cove where the detail gouge (the normal tool for beads and coves) cannot reach, the short point can be used at the bottom of the cove. There, the back of the tool bevel can be held against the cove wall to act as a pivot point when the tool is twisted slightly. In doing this, the short point cuts a narrow arc at the bottom of the cove.

The skew is a tool that most beginner turners tend to shy away from, especially once they experience their first big dig-in. However, it is well worth persevering with because of the quality finish you can achieve with it.

❯ Using the flat of the skew to execute a planing cut that leaves a very clean finish. Only the bottom third of the blade is used. Note also, the fine shavings on my hand.

Using the skew on its side on the tool rest to clean up and straighten the sides of a wine bottle coaster and to mark grooves in the base of a bowl.

Using scrapers

Scrapers are amongst the oldest of the turning tools and are perhaps the easiest and safest for the beginner to learn to use. They are flat bars of steel (carbon or high-speed steel), the tips of which are ground to the desired shape. The ground shape gives each scraper its name: flat nose scraper; round nose; half-round. Thickness of the steel bar varies from around $\frac{5}{32}$in to $\frac{1}{2}$in (4 to 12mm) and the tools can vary in width from $\frac{1}{2}$ to 1in (12 to 25mm). The thicker the steel, the more robust and stable the tool will be and the heavier the work it will be able to do.

Every time I start using a scraper, it is taken to the grinder and given a quick touch-up. Some say that the grinding process produces a fine burr or wire on the edge of the scraper and it is this wire that does the cutting. Others argue that it is the sharp edge that cuts. Either way, when sharp, a scraper works very efficiently and it can be used to remove large quantities of waste material quite rapidly from end-grain and cross-grain work. It can also be used gently to smooth lines and produce a nice finish on hollowed work, the inside and outside walls of bowls or even on long, flowing lines and coves in spindle work.

The secret to using scrapers is to raise the tool rest slightly and hold the tool flat on the tool rest so the back of the handle is slightly higher than the tip that is connecting the wood at about centre height. This enables the scraper to do what its name suggests – scrape off layers of wood. If a catch occurs, all that will happen is the tip will be forced down and out of the wood. If the handle is allowed to drop below the height of the tip, the tip will chatter against the wood spinning down against it and dig-ins are more likely to occur.

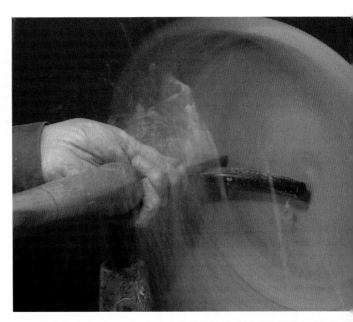

Using a half-round nose scraper to remove waste from the bottom of a fairly large bowl. Raise the tool rest slightly and hold the back of the handle higher than the blade. In this picture, waste material is still being removed. However, the scraper can be used to execute fine finishing cuts.

When the flat nose scraper is used for robust end-grain hollowing of vessels or for removal of waste in cross-grain work, it is advisable to drill a central pilot hole first so that the whole width of the scraper is not in contact with the wood at once (see pages 101 and 176). Starting from the edge of the pilot hole so that less than half the scraper is in contact with the wood, push straight in towards the headstock. Material should be removed fairly smoothly and rapidly. As you work close to the centre, it is possible that the bottom corner of the scraper may rub against the wood curving around underneath and push the scraper towards the centre as you push it in. Provided the tool isn't pushed against the wood spinning up on the back of the lathe, don't worry. As you make successive cuts towards the outside of the vessel, the circle you have cut will widen out and the bottom corner will be less likely to connect. Try raising the tool rest slightly to give you more clearance for the tool.

The round nose or half-round scraper can also be used to remove waste material as above, but is more likely to be used for finishing work – smoothing lines and rough cuts inside hollowed pieces and on the inside and outside of bowls. With the tool flat on the tool rest and the handle higher than the tip, move the tool across the wood so that the grain fibres that are being cut are supported by grain behind it. This is a very light-handed action.

For finishing cuts, scrapers can also be used with the tool held on its side on the tool rest and moved around the wood at a 45° angle to the wood. This is known as a shear scrape or shear cut and produces fine sawdust or fine, curly shavings.

Using the parting tool

Use this tool to part off work, cut spigots and to turn flat sections on spindle work. It can be used in two ways. First, it can be held on the tool rest and pushed almost horizontally into the wood – a bit like a scraper. It works, but the cut you will get might not be very clean, and you will blunt the tool fairly quickly.

The second technique is to hold the handle much lower and move the tool into the spinning wood so that the bottom bevel is rubbing and the blade is planing off thin shavings. This will give you a cleaner cut, far less chatter, and the tool will stay sharp for longer.

Using the parting tool to face off end-grain spindle work.

Planing off thin shavings from the wood – the most efficient way to use the parting tool.

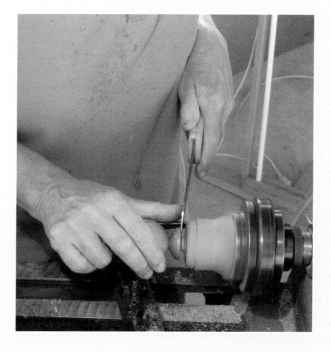

▶ **Parting off spindle work. The left hand is holding the tool close to the body. The right hand is stable on the tool rest and cradling the spinning work. The right thumb is stabilizing the tool, which is angled slightly to undercut the base so the concave surface will sit stable on the table.**

88

Projects

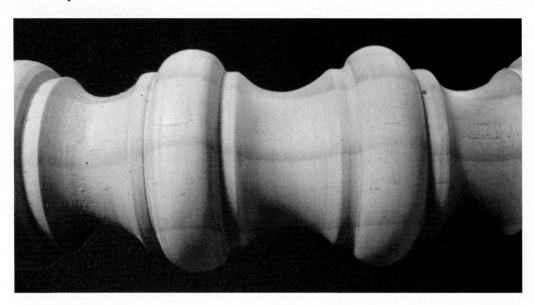

Beads, fillets and coves.

Project 1: Spindle work – beads, fillets and coves

To turn beads on spindle work, first turn the piece down to a cylinder, then mark and cut a series of lines approximately ½in (13mm) apart. To do this just hold a ruler next to the wood and mark the positions on the wood with a pencil as the wood is spinning. The next step is to use these lines as a guide for cutting grooves that will be the low points on either side of the beads.

Using the skew chisel to cut grooves

The grooves can be done with the skew chisel. You can also cut them with the detail gouge but the skew chisel is best. Start with the skew blade held vertically, long point down on the tool rest, at 90° to the spinning wood, and the handle held close in against your body. Holding the blade vertically is important because if you have the tool twisted slightly, it will skim along the wood rather than plunge cut in. Advance the tool into the marked wood, while at the same time lifting the back of the tool. This is like a plunge cut. Withdraw the tool as soon as the cut is made, with a smooth, but short, sharp action.

Marking ½in (13mm) intervals on the spinning cylinder.

◄ Cutting grooves with the skew.

You don't want the wood or the tool to burn. Work all the way along the cylinder and you should have developed a rhythm by the time you get to the end.

Using the detail or spindle gouge to form beads

The grooves cut by the skew form the lowest points at either side of the bead. With the detail gouge, you will be doing two cuts to create one side of the bead, then two on the opposite side. Place the gouge on the rest with the flute so that it faces straight up at you. Advance the tool onto the work so that the heel of the bevel first touches approximately $\frac{3}{32}$in (2mm) in from one of the grooves. Raise the back of the handle until the point starts to cut. In a smooth movement, roll the tool sideways and then push gently in (while still rolling) towards the bottom of the groove. This should take off the sharp edge of the groove and be the beginning of one side of a nice, rounded bead.

Start a second cut halfway between both grooves and repeat the rolling and pushing action. You are aiming for a nice, convex curve. Use your body to help get the roll right and make sure that the bevel is rubbing on the wood throughout the cut. These techniques enable greater tool control and help to produce a neat shape and finish.

Once the first side of the bead is finished, work towards the second groove using the same process to complete your bead.

1–**2** Starting the first side of the bead: with the flute facing up; rolling and pushing while the bevel is rubbing and ending with the flute facing sideways in the groove.

90

1–**2** Completing the bead by repeating the rolling action in the opposite direction towards the next groove.

3–**5** Using the parting tool to flatten out beads to create fillets.

The next step is to practise. Using the marks on the wood as a guide, turn beads along the whole length of the piece. Repetition of the process cements the movements in the brain, and your movements become much more automatic and fluid. Hopefully, your beads at the end of the piece will be better than those at the beginning.

Using the parting tool to create fillets

Once you get the feel of how to do the beads correctly, it's time to create fillets – those neat little flat pieces that often come between a bead and a cove. These are done with a parting tool, leaving one bead, wiping out the next two beads and leaving the third one, all along the wood.

I have seen the parting tool being used in two different ways by turners. The first way is to use it as a scraper – to push the edge of the tool straight into the wood with the handle held almost horizontally. Provided the tool is sharp, this method works but it will blunt the tool fairly quickly and may rip the grain on the wood. The second way, to use the parting tool to execute a shearing or planing cut, is a better method.

Starting with the handle down low, rub the bevel on the wood to be cut. Then, keeping the tool still on the tool rest, gently lift the back of the handle until the tool edge starts to cut. You will be planing layers off the wood as it rotates on the lathe and it will be a smooth action. As you plane down into the cylinder, you may have to lift the back of the tool handle gradually to maintain the cut. Doing this, remove two out of every three beads until you have a series of flat areas that are twice the width of the beads between them.

Marking the edge of the fillets and the centre.

Using the detail gouge to create coves

Use a pencil to mark the centre of each flat section. This mark indicates where the centre of each cove will be.

To turn a cove on spindle work, the gouge is held so that the flute is at 90° to the turner, facing the direction in which the cove will be gouged out. Start the cut left of centre with the sweet point of the gouge (which is the top part of the lady's fingernail – on this part of the tool you won't get any kickback).

Once the sweet point has entered the wood, you have a shoulder on which to support the bevel. Next, push in and towards what will be the centre of the cove at the same time rolling the tool so that at the end of the cut (the bottom of the cove), the flute of the tool is facing up. The bevel should be rubbing throughout the cut. The movement is the opposite of what you do when turning a bead.

Starting the cove left of the centre mark with the flute facing towards centre between the two beads.

▶ The gouge is pushed in and rolled so that the flute finishes facing up.

Make a number of passes from opposite sides to open the cove out until the pencil marks for the edges of the fillets are reached.

Do not attempt to push the tool up and out the other side, as you will then be cutting unsupported grain. Lift the tool and make a second similar cut coming from the opposite direction. You may need to make two or three passes from each side to get the depth and width of cove you want. Leave a little flat bit (the fillet) either side of each bead.

Continue practising all the way along the piece. Once you have mastered the movement for beads, fillets and coves, you have the basics for almost all spindle work. Everything else is just a variation on that theme.

Making the second cut from the opposite side, starting with the flute facing the centre of the cove and again finishing with it facing up.

Project 2:
Turning a small vase

The techniques employed in this project are
similar to the beads and coves exercise, but also
take you into other ways of using the skew,
drilling on the lathe, using the bowl gouge and
parting a piece right off the lathe.

The finished vase.

Mount a block of wood approximately 2in (50mm) square
and 4³⁄₄–5¹⁄₂in (120–140mm) long into the chuck. Using the
skew chisel on its side, make small cuts into the centre of
the end grain to establish the mouth of the vase and make
a definite starting point when drilling.

▶ Mount the Jacob's chuck and drill in the tailstock, slow
the lathe down and wind the drill in to the desired depth.
Pull the drill out at intervals and clear it of waste. Remove
the Jacob's chuck and replace the tailstock point.

You will need a cone-shaped tailstock point for this project. I didn't have one when I was using this little lathe, so had to make one.

Use the large bowl gouge or the roughing gouge to turn the blank down to a cylinder. Note that in all the photos where a gouge is being used, the bevel behind the cutting edge is in contact with the wood. This helps support the tool and prevents dig-ins. Keep the bevel rubbing.

Test for round and then, still using the large bowl gouge, remove waste material along the length of what will be the neck of the vase.

Change to a detail gouge to tidy up the rim of the vase mouth and start refining the upper neck of the vase.

When cutting the neck and upper part of the bulb in the vase, aim for a smooth-flowing curve. The finer the neck, the better the piece will look. You may find clearing the waste and shaping the long curve of the neck easier with the bowl gouge. It is a more solid tool with a shorter bevel.

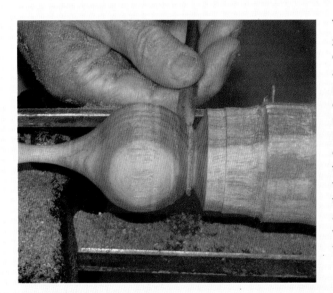

You can either continue with the detail gouge or the bowl gouge to refine the shape of the vase bulb about two-thirds of the way down. The bowl gouge will be the more solid and stable tool to use. As you shape the bottom of the bulb, you will have to remove some waste, then refine the curve. It is like cutting a large bead. Keep the bevel rubbing and the tool tucked into your body and move your body to create the curve. Once you get further round the curve, and as you remove more waste, you will be shaping the top of the foot as well as the bottom of the bulb. You will need to change to a detail or spindle gouge to get into the tighter curve. Cutting is always downhill, so that you are always cutting supported wood grains, similar to the way you would do the beads and coves. Start forming the foot closer to the headstock.

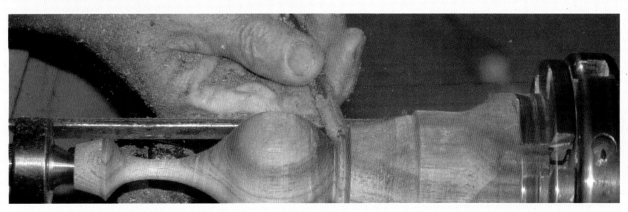

Use a parting tool to cut in about 1/8in (3mm) and establish the bottom of the foot. The detail gouge can then be used to round over and tidy it up. You musn't make the foot too thin, as the end grain will split.

Further refine the shape of the foot. Consider its size in relation to the rest of the vase at this point.

Sand, keeping the edges sharp and the curves smooth. Don't roll the sandpaper over the edges. Keep the sandpaper moving to prevent scratches.

Apply your chosen finish. In this case, it is a lacquer-based sanding sealer applied with a rag, with the lathe turning very slowly. Once applied, quickly wipe off the excess and buff the work up.

Parting the piece off while supporting it with the right hand.

If there is a little pip in the centre of the base, remove it with a knife then do the final sanding of the base using Velcro-backed sandpaper on a power sanding attachment. These are available commercially or you can make your own (see chapter 15, 'Using Jigs'). Work through the grits from 120 to 400 (see chapter 9, 'Sanding'). Apply your chosen finish to the base and the job is done.

Project 3:
Turning a wine bottle coaster

I use a set of cardboard discs held in the centre with drawing pins to give me the circle and the centre. The blank should be about 1in (25mm) wider in diameter than the bottom of a wide wine bottle. Keep hands well clear of the band saw blade when cutting.

For small projects like this one, a screw chuck can be used. This one has a home-made shim on it to reduce its length. Drill a central hole with a slightly smaller diameter than that of the screw, leaving ½–⅝in (13–15mm) clearance in the bottom. Holding the headstock still, screw the prepared blank on.

Bring the tailstock up for extra support while roughing out. Use a bowl gouge to bring the sides down to round. The finishing cuts can be done in a shear cutting action with the tool on its side and handle down low.

Face off the bottom. This can be done either with a shear cutting action from centre out, or from outside in.

◄ Lay a tool across the base to ensure that the surface is slightly concave.

► A small scraper, ground at an angle to give the dovetail, is used to cut a recess for the chuck to grip. I have ground an old woodworking chisel for this purpose. Check the width of the chuck jaws to find the size you need to make the recess. Do not make the recess too deep or you will have to leave too much wood in the base later on.

Sand, working through the grits 120, 180, 240, 320 and 400 and apply your finish. Because this will hold a bottle that might be wet, I have selected a lacquer-based sanding sealer mixed 50/50 with thinners and later on a spray with lacquer. I brush it on, wipe off the excess immediately with the lathe stationary, then buff it up with the work spinning.

Unscrew the piece from the screw chuck, remove that, then reverse the piece and grip it in the chuck jaws ready for hollowing out.

Use a square nose scraper to remove the inside waste, starting from the inside screw hole and working out. Hold the tool parallel with the lathe bed and with the back of the handle higher than the cutting edge. You will probably have to raise the tool rest for the scraper.

Gently push the tool into the wood. If possible, use only half, or less than half, of the tool edge for each pass. The less the tool has to cut, the easier it is. Remove the waste until you have got to the bottom of the drill hole.

Check the thickness of the base by using your thumb on the tool inside, then outside the coaster wall.

Use the long point of the skew with the skew on its side on the tool rest to clean down and make the side walls vertical, and to cut a couple of decorative grooves in the bottom. The bottom should be slightly concave so that the wine bottle will sit in it without rocking.

Sand and apply the finish to the inside of the coaster. That's it!

What grits to use and how to use them effectively

Sandpaper comes in a range of grits from about 16 grit (boulders on paper!) right through to 2,500 grit wet-and-dry paper which is used mainly to finish paint work on a car. It is good to have a selection of grits on hand. For most uses, you will need 120, 180, 240, 320 and 400 grit. However, 80 and 100 grit paper is sometimes handy when there are stubborn lumps and bumps or torn end grain, which just will not settle down with the standard treatment. The finer grits – 600, 800. 1,000, 1,200, 1,500, 2,000 and 2,500, which are mostly available as wet-and-dry paper – are good if you want that special finish on a piece. Once you work through these grits, the sanded piece just feels so nice and smooth and it glows, even before you apply the finish. The pleasure of feeling wood sanded to 2,500 grit is often worth the extra bit of effort. These finer grits can be used if you are applying an oil finish, between or during the application of each coat of oil. They can also be used when lacquering a piece, between successive coats of lacquer. Used wet with a little bit of soap as a lubricant, the fine sandpaper removes any irregularities caused by dust adhering with the lacquer. Make sure the soap and water is wiped off and dry before the next coat of lacquer is applied.

The best type of paper to get is cloth-backed paper, which is usually sold in 4oft (12m) rolls. When you get the rolls, mark the back of them with a thick felt pen as follows: 120 grit – no mark; 180 grit – one thick line along the full length of the roll; 240 grit – two thick lines; 320 grit – three thick lines; 400 grit – four thick lines. When you need the sandpaper, tear off strips from every roll and stack them together in order, with 120 grit on top and 400 grit on the bottom. Keep the pieces together with a bulldog clip or a large paper clip.

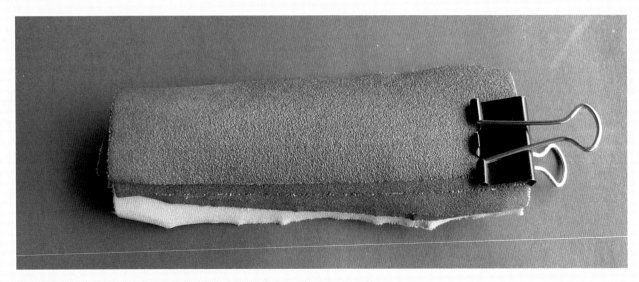

Keep the grits together, coarsest on top, with a bulldog clip or paper clip.

Sanding spindle work. Support delicate pieces with your free hand. Only sand one face at a time and do not sand over the sharp edges. Keep the edges crisp. If you are holding all the strips of sandpaper in a bulldog clip, when one grit is used, it can be folded back and the finer grit underneath is exposed for use. When sanding spindle work, hold one end of the strips (or the bulldog clip holding the strips) in one hand and support the paper on the wood with your other hand. You don't need to press hard. Let the sandpaper do the work. Keep the paper moving across the work, as there are high, sharp points on the paper, and if you hold it still on one point, these high points will scratch the wood.

If you are sanding spindle work with nice sharp edges, don't sand those edges away. Take the paper up to the edge, lift it, change angle and continue further along. There are some parts of spindle work, which, if tooled nicely with a skew, might only need a light touch with 400 grit. It doesn't need anything coarser than that.

When you are satisfied that you have got the marks and scratches out with 120 grit, move on to the next finer grit. Don't skip grits, as all the scratches from the coarser sandpaper won't have been worked out. Turn the lathe off after the first couple of grits to make sure you are getting all the scratches out, as they won't come out once you move to the finer grits. The finer grits do more polishing than removing of scratches.

106

Using a drill-mounted power sander with the drill and the lathe going at the same time. Slow the lathe down, hold the drill close to the body for support and keep the sander at a slight angle to the work so that not the entire sanding disc touches the wood at the same time. If it does, it will kick.

Once the sandpaper starts getting blunt or clogged, get a fresh piece. Blunt sandpaper is like blunt tools, and does more damage than good.

When sanding bowl work, where there is a large surface with no detail, it is possible to speed up the sanding process by using a power sanding attachment that is held in an electric drill. Velcro-backed sandpaper discs are attached to the top of the attachment and, with the drill and the lathe running (slower than turning speed), the sandpaper is moved across the work in much the same way as you would by hand.

You can also use a hand-held rotary sander, which works on the same principle as the drill and power sanding attachment except that it relies on the spinning of the bowl to give it the rotary action. They are effective, although much gentler than the drill.

The power sanding attachment can also be held in a chuck and used to sand the bases of vases, boxes and similar spindle work projects.

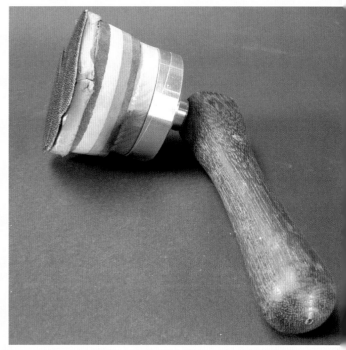

A home-made rotary sander made from a turned handle; a video head, complete with bearings cannibalized from an old VCR unit; an old sandal and some Velcro. Commercial ones are also available.

Dealing with torn end grain

Torn end grain shows itself as a rough, uneven surface, which, no matter how carefully you sand, doesn't seem to want to smooth out. It occurs mostly on the surface of a bowl in soft, open-grain wood, where you are cutting the end grain of the timber, particularly where the grain isn't well supported.

Good tool work is your first line of defence. Once the shaping of the outside and the hollowing work on the inside is done, it is a good idea to touch up the gouge or scraper that you are using so that your final cuts are made with a good, sharp tool.

On the outside, where you are most likely to be using a bowl gouge, make your final cuts from the base to rim so that the grain is being supported as you cut. The cuts should be smooth and fine and the bevel of the gouge should be rubbing. Keep the tool handle tucked into your body and move your whole body to produce a smooth movement. Try a shear cut with the handle down low, bevel rubbing and the sharp edge on the side of the gouge (flute almost unseen) presenting to the work. You should get very fine, curly shavings or just dust coming off.

The width and depth of the bowl and whether the rim is undercut or not, will determine whether you will be finishing the inside with a bowl gouge or with a round nose scraper. Either way, your cuts will also need to be smooth and fine.

If your tool work is the best you can manage, and there is still torn end grain, you may need to start sanding with a coarser grit than normal – perhaps 80 grit. Even then, perseverance is the key. Don't move on to a finer grit until you are satisfied that the coarser grit has removed all the roughness. The power sanding attachment in a drill (with the lathe slowed down a bit) will speed up this sort of sanding work. Turn the lathe off after each grit and check to see that the roughness has been sanded away.

If the torn end grain is still there, try stabilizing the offending area with sanding sealer or superglue (cyanoacrylate) and work through the grits again. Patience has to win out in the end!

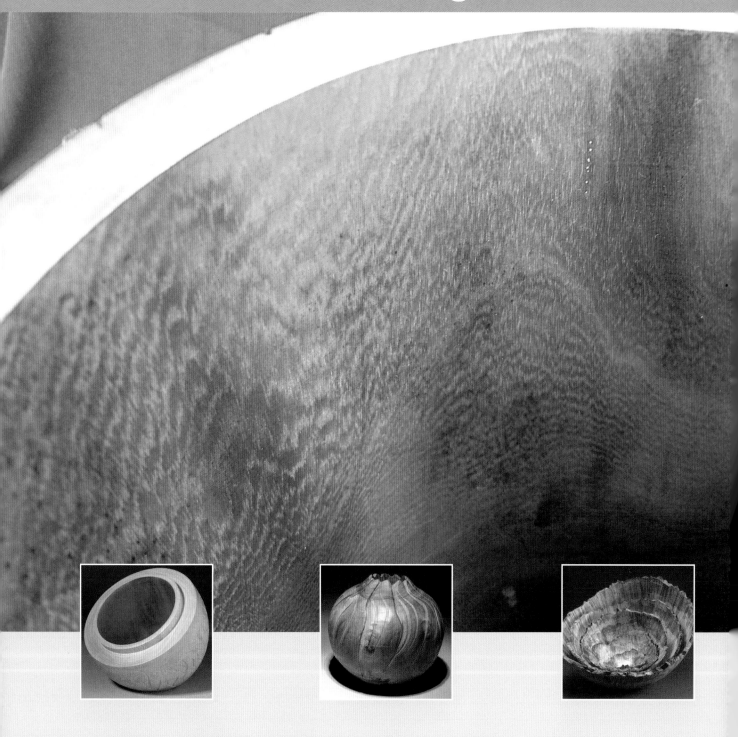

10
Finishing

Using stains and dyes on wood

There is a great range of stains and wood dyes on the market. Most of them are either spirit- or water-based. Bitter experience has made me shy away from using spirit-based stains on turning. They dry quickly, often unevenly, and show up every little scratch or blemish in the wood – even ones you didn't see before applying the stain. Not all finishes (oils, waxes, lacquers) go well over stains, as they tend to bleed into the finish. I wouldn't recommend using them. However, if you do choose to, make sure you read the instructions on the can and prepare your work thoroughly.

Water-based dyes are much easier to use. You can get a range of colours from the muted natural wood hues to some quite outrageous shades. These water dyes soak into the wood and are translucent so you can still see the wood grain. They may also be diluted or colours blended together.

Different products will be available in different countries. There are water-based dyes produced specifically for wood that come either in powder or liquid form. They are generally quite strong and produce a vibrant colour, especially on pale wood.

Other water-based dyes not necessarily produced for wood can also be used, such as food colourings, which are amongst my favourites. Undiluted, these colours are very rich. They are generally available in four colours – cochineal pink, blue, green and yellow – from most supermarkets. Find yourself a cake-decorating supplier and you can get dozens of different colours. Provided the finished piece is not subjected to very bright light or direct sunlight, the colours stay fast.

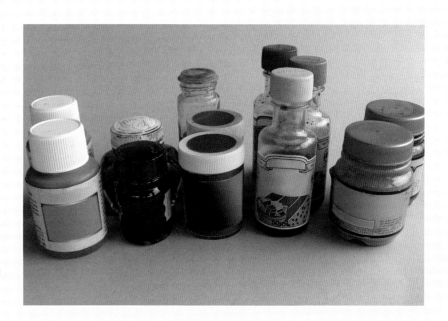

From left to right: non-toxic water dyes produced specifically for wood; black and red inks; fabric dyes in powder form, mixed with water in the bottle behind; food colourings; silk paints (dyes).

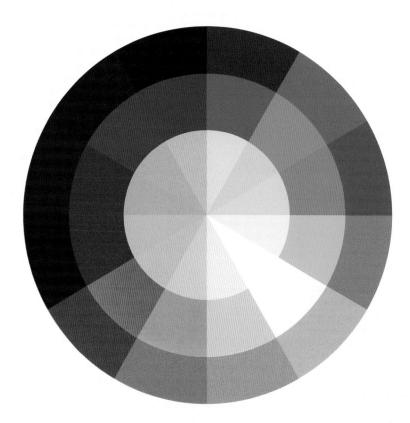

Analogous colours are those next to each other on the wheel; complementary colours are opposites. Analogous colours in water-based dyes look best when blended next to each other. Try to blend complementary colours and you will get a muddy brown. Try using a base of water-based dye in one colour (such as blue), dry it, and then put a small touch of opaque paint (acrylic or enamel) in a complementary colour (such as warm yellow or orange) over part of that and you should get a pleasing effect.

Cloth dye and silk paints can also be used. Cloth dye comes in powder or liquid form. Use the liquid form undiluted. When you mix the powder with water, use only a small amount of water to dissolve the dye, then try it on some scrap wood. You can then dilute it if necessary, but it's a lot harder to sort out if you mix it too weak to start with. The silk paints to use are really dyes and have a consistency not unlike water. Avoid fabric paints that have a thicker consistency and are designed to sit on the fabric. What you want are the ones that soak in. With certain brands, the colours in these are superb.

When preparing to apply the dyes, first sand the piece to at least 400 grit. Further sanding with finer grades will enhance your finish. Wet

the piece with a brush or wet rag to raise the grain and sand again. One turner I know rubs the work with a rag generously soaked in methylated spirits (denatured alcohol). It raises the grain, but dries more quickly than water.

Wet the piece again and brush on the dye. Keep it wet as you work so that brush strokes blend into each other. For special colour effects

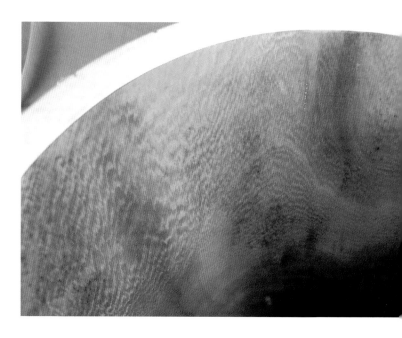

in certain areas, you can gently blend colours into each other. Colours which are analogous (they are next to each other on the colour wheel, such as blue and green; blue and violet) are best done this way. Complementary colours (opposites on the colour wheel, such as blue and orange; purple and yellow) will only blend to form a muddy brown.

Once you are satisfied with the colour, let the piece dry and then apply your favourite finish. Oils, waxes, polyurethanes, lacquers and resins will all go over a water-based dye.

The inside of this jacaranda bowl is coloured with yellow, green and blue food colouring. The combined blue and yellow areas ended up as a slightly different green. There was already some spalting in the bowl before the colouring. This shows through as the darker lines. The aim was to get the colours to blend into each other – so no sharp edges of colour – yet still be distinct.

▶ Fig vase coloured in blue food dye and violet and crimson silk dyes (analogous colours). The collar at the top was sprayed with copper enamel paint (a complementary colour). Fig is naturally a light colour with a very pronounced pattern of growth rings. These show through the dyes.

◀ Pumpkin pot. Turned, carved and coloured with food dyes.

There is a great range of wood finishing products on the market. Not one of them is ideal for every purpose. They all have their advantages and disadvantages. This section offers a review of each group of finishes, with an overview of their characteristics, suggesting when best to use them and giving some ideas on how to apply them.

Oils

The advantage of oils is that they are very easy to use and can be applied on or off the lathe. Good application of oil is, however, time consuming. Oils penetrate the wood and have a preserving effect. Used over time on green turned wood, oil will replace moisture and help prevent checking and cracking. To apply, simply brush or rub on with a rag or sponge, turn on the lathe and buff the piece up. This can be done two or three times to increase the amount and penetration of oil in the piece. Once the piece is off the lathe, it pays to wipe it over with an oily rag and buff a couple more times, leaving at least 24 hours between applications. Application instructions vary from one product to another, so make sure you read the instructions on the can. After about twenty minutes, if any oil is still sitting on the surface of the wood then wipe it off – otherwise it goes sticky. If you find imperfections in the work, you can re-sand with sandpaper lubricated with oil, then re-apply the finish.

The contents in oil finishing products vary. Usually it is an oil base, such as linseed oil, tung oil, orange peel oil or walnut oil, combined with thinners and drying agents. I am told that a lot of the Danish oils have polyurethane in them to make them harden. It is the thinners, drying agents and hardeners that you need to be aware of – always check the contents label, recommended uses and instructions on the can. With some oils, once the can has been opened and some of the contents used, exposure to air will cause the remains in the tin to gel. Either decant the contents into smaller bottles and seal them or put marbles in the oil can to raise the oil level and exclude the air. Putting the smaller bottles in the refrigerator can also help. Make sure that you label all containers clearly, or the consequences could be disastrous.

Thinners and drying agents in oils can also be very volatile and quite toxic. Ensure the area where you are using them is well ventilated and wear rubber gloves. When finished, do not leave used oil rags in a pile in the workshop or they may spontaneously combust. Rinse all rags out and hang them out to dry.

Less toxic oil finishes are also available. These mostly use lead-free driers, lemon and orange peel oil, linseed oil and paraffin oil. The ingredients are usually derived from plants.

Tip

The better the preparation, the better the finish you will get. Sand to at least 400 grit. For special pieces, change over to wet-and-dry sandpaper after 400 grit and work through the grits to 2,500 grit. By this stage, the wood should glow even before any finish is applied.

'Siblings'. The beautiful sheen on these maple burl bowls was obtained with three or four coats of oil.

Check the description on the labels. Any food grade oil which doesn't readily oxidize – the polyunsaturated types – can also be used on food serving items such as salad and fruit bowls, spatulas and spoons, spoon jars, cutting boards and pot stands. However, there is the danger of these attracting dust and encouraging mould growth in damp weather. Baby oil, which is a mineral oil, can also be used. I use this on foot massage rollers and some children's toys, but not on food items.

Most oil finishes will give you a matt or a low sheen finish. They do need some maintenance and a lot of them tend to attract dust. Oils can be used under a wax finish, but not on top of one, as the solvents in the oil may dissolve the wax underneath and leave dirty, dull streaks.

Finishing

Wax

Most wood waxes on the market contain either beeswax, which is a very soft wax; carnauba, which is a very hard and durable wax; or can have a mixture of the two. They may also contain solvents, perfumes and colour.

The beauty of waxes is that they are easy to apply on the lathe. Once sanding is done, apply the wax on a clean cloth with the work stationary, then turn the lathe on and buff. Apply some pressure as the friction causes the wax to melt and penetrate the wood, and that's it – done! One wax product, a pen wax that comes in a very hard bar, is simply rubbed on the spinning pen and buffed up. The lathe doesn't even have to be stopped. Another wax product, Shellawax, designed specifically for turning, contains shellac and waxes, which produces a brilliant sheen. However, because it contains shellac, it is not water resistant and may dull down in hot and humid conditions.

Waxes can be used over almost all other finishes although it pays to check the product information before trying it. Provided the preparation has been thorough, the end result is a beautiful finish that glows and has a smooth, sensual feel.

The downside to waxes is that they do need some maintenance. Over time, especially when the piece is handled regularly or if it is in an area where there are extreme weather conditions – such as heat, high or low humidity – a wax finish will dull and need further buffing. With this in mind, wax is best used on 'show' or decorative pieces which aren't handled a lot and which you don't mind giving a bit of a rub occasionally.

Shellac

Shellac comes from the hard coating of the lac beetle and is the material used in traditional French polishing. It usually comes in flakes and has to be dissolved in denatured alcohol (white spirit or methylated spirits). You can also get it ready mixed. The most readily available shellac, orange shellac, has a slightly honeyed colour. This is imparted to the wood. You can also get blonde shellac if you don't want extra colour on the finish. It can be applied with a brush or cloth rubber with the lathe stationary and then buffed. If desired, it can then be cut back lightly with a very fine grit sandpaper and then reapplied and buffed. This process is the basis of French polishing. What you are doing is slowly filling the low points and sanding off the high points. It is very time consuming, but the results are exquisite.

Shellac is not water resistant: a splash of water will leave a white mark on the work. It is best used on small decorative pieces or under other finishes, such as waxes, lacquers or epoxy resins. Shellac flakes need to be kept cool. Heat and humidity may cause the product to go waxy or oily when diluted.

Lacquers, varnishes and resins

These finishes are grouped together as, unlike the oils and waxes, they produce a hard coat on the surface rather than penetrating into the wood. The advantage of these finishes is that they are quick and easy to apply with the work off the lathe and the finish is a hard, durable one that doesn't need any maintenance. For this reason, I use lacquers extensively for small, decorative and functional items to be sold through retail outlets – items such as potpourri bowls, fragrance flasks, handles for magnifying glasses and knives, wine bottle stoppers, calendar, clock and barometer surrounds and wine bottle coasters. Over time however, it can get scratched, and the wood to be coated does need to be fully seasoned.

Spraying lacquer outside using a car touch-up gun. Lacquer spray can do harm to your lungs and be absorbed through the skin. Do not spray in the workshop or a confined room. If you have the luxury of a spray booth, use it. If not, work outside, check the way the breeze is blowing, cover up and wear an appropriate mask. Lacquering cannot be done when the humidity is high. The surface sprayed will go dull or milky. If it is getting late in the day or looks like rain, leave the lacquering until another day.

Lacquer can be purchased in different levels of gloss – usually 30, 70 or 100 per cent gloss (produced by adding more or less talc to the lacquer). Thinners are also needed and a spray system – an air compressor and spray gun – is necessary to apply it. For small items, a tiny spray bottle works well; for larger items, I use a car touch-up gun. The lacquer and thinners are mixed, about 50/50. Spraying must be done either outside or in a spray booth and a mask must always be used – lacquer down the lungs is dangerous. Also avoid windy or dusty areas. With the compressor set between 30 and 50 psi, spray with a slow, even motion, backwards and forwards or up and down. Do not hold the gun still on the one spot or you will get runs. If you are going to be doing a lot of lacquering, setting up a swivel arrangement with an old office chair or a slowly revolving motor makes it possible to spray the whole piece evenly. It also means that you view the whole piece in the same light which is important.

Lacquer will tack off in a few minutes and dry in about two hours, after which you can sand back, wipe and apply a further coat. To get the finest finish after your last spray, sand it back with fine grit sandpaper or steel wool and then buff up with a wax. You'll be able to see your face in it. One common problem encountered with spraying lacquer is clogging of the spray nozzle or the small breather hole in the lid. A spray with thinners usually clears the nozzle. A pin can be used to relieve the breather hole. I was once told that when it comes to spraying lacquer with spray bottles and guns, cleanliness comes before godliness. I guess it depends on your perspective.

Varnishes also produce a hard surface that is good on toys or games. They can be applied with a brush, rag or sprayed. I have seen varnish applied to lamp stands and bowls, but it looked thick, sludgy and not very nice. It needs thinning down before applying and should be applied using a number of thin coats rather than one thick one. One disadvantage of varnishes is the drying time, which is at least a few hours and long enough for plenty of dust to get trapped and make the finish a second-rate one. However there are some quick-drying varnishes on the market now.

Resins come in two parts, which are mixed together before use. Once mixed, the hardening process begins so only mix what you need.

If you happen to mix up too much for a job, you can, with some brands, get away with storing it in the refrigerator for about twenty-four hours, but label it clearly and check with the 'kitchen boss' first. Resins can be sprayed or applied with a brush or rag. Use rubber gloves and a mask when handling resins and check the manufacturer's specifications for drying times.

Food-safe finishes

Taking into account the characteristics of all these finishes, it could be concluded that oils (only those with the food-safe label), then beeswax and resins (fully cured) can be used on food serving items and children's toys. However, when it comes to using wooden items for food serving purposes, I tend to be very careful and employ the motto: 'When in doubt, don't!' I don't put a salad covered in mayonnaise or vinegar dressing in a wooden bowl.

Common sense in the use and care of wooden food serving items, such as cooking spatulas and spoons, salad servers, cutting boards, pot stands and bowls, also needs to be employed. Wash the items in hot, soapy water, but don't leave them to soak. Wipe them dry and store them in an airy place so they don't get mould growing on them. Don't put them in the microwave or dishwasher. Common sense, yes, but we still need the occasional reminder.

Goblets by Bob Cargill. Bob uses a very fine-bristled make-up brush to apply eight coats of thinned-down resin (two pot plastic), leaving eight hours between coats (playing it safe) and sanding very lightly between every coat. The result is a beautiful mirror-like finish. After leaving them to cure for thirty days, Bob and his family do drink wine from these goblets, but he wouldn't recommend 'leaving the wine dregs in overnight'. The acid in the wine might eat through the finish.

Part Three

Advanced Techniques

11

Planning and Designing a Piece

A few years ago, I was in a pottery class with a number of us all working at our own pieces around the room. At one point during the day, a middle-aged lady with a very posh accent suddenly gushed out to everybody and nobody in particular, "Oh, I just want to make the most beautiful things!" Our instructor very quietly went over to her and replied, "Yes dear, that's what we're all here for." I smiled inwardly.

So saying, in our woodturning, we also all aim to make pieces that are, maybe not gushily beautiful, but nevertheless pleasing to the eye, whether they be bowls, candle holders, vases, vessels or sculptural pieces. Unfortunately, we don't always hit the mark when it comes to making 'the most beautiful things' (or the most interesting or intriguing), and second-hand shops often have an array of turned wooden objects which someone has laboured hard over, but hasn't quite got it right with their form, finish or design.

We can identify a number of features that should make a piece pleasing or captivating to the eye of the viewer. These would include: the wood; the finish; the form and the design. Although there is not a formula, a combination of the right piece of wood, a well-executed finish appropriate to the piece, clean form and a well-planned and well-executed design should bring us close to the piece we are proud of. Each of these aspects will be considered in turn.

A well designed and well executed sculptural piece, which has interesting front and back views.

122

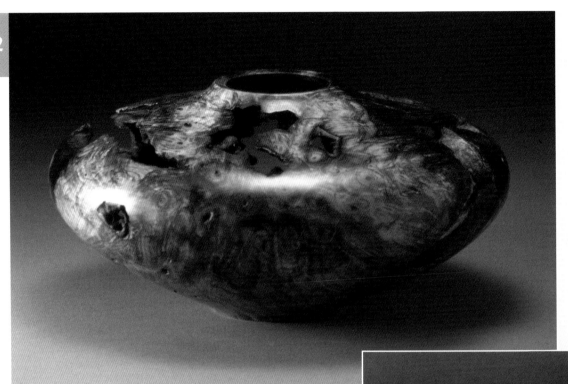

Stunning wood; simple design. Buckeye burl hollow form.

▶▶ **Urn in jacaranda, kwila and red cedar. Although the blonde jacaranda does exhibit some grain pattern, it is generally a fairly bland timber – a good choice to enable the lamination in this urn to be emphasized.**

The wood

When a woodturner of only a few years' experience, I once found myself at a wood show admiring the pieces that another turner had on display. I spent quite a lot of time drooling over his work. However, there was one piece that my eyes were constantly being drawn back to. It was a small bowl, a very simple shape, but nevertheless beautiful. Seeing me standing there for so long and fondling this bowl, the turner must have thought he had a definite sale on his hands.

My mind then went from envy mode to analysis. What was it that made me like that bowl? The shape was simple. With a bit of care, I could and did do that. The finish was subtle and well executed. With patience, I could also do that. What it boiled down to was the wood. The colour and grain were exquisite. For something as simple as that bowl, the wood was an excellent choice. That is why burls (or burrs) and highly figured timbers are so popular among woodturners. The work can be simple, but the wood can be stunning. So, our choice of wood is important.

However, there are also times when a very bland timber is necessary so that the design or the surface decoration stands out. In some cases a very nasty piece of wood – one with large checks, rot, weathering and bark inclusions – may be appropriate for the design. The timber needs to be suited to the piece being planned and vice versa.

Decorated bowls in kauri pine. The relatively bland wood is a good choice for the applied decoration.

Burl bowl. The curves are smooth with no jarring flats or bumps.

The finish

The quality and appropriateness of a finish is essential when you are aiming to produce a quality piece. Most turners seem to go through a process of trying a lot of different finishing materials, then settling for one or two with which they are most comfortable. Once you are familiar with your chosen finishes, you know what they will do and how to apply them to get the best results; it is simply a matter of putting in the time, care and patience to get a result as close to perfect as possible. This involves using fine finishing cuts before sanding, working through all the sandpaper grits to the finest grits available, checking regularly in good light throughout the sanding process to see that all scratches are being removed, carefully going back over the work if necessary and, finally, careful and thorough application of the finish.

French polishing techniques, such as multiple applications of the finish interspersed with fine cutting back and final rubbing and buffing, can be employed. Seeing woodworkers putting final, careful finishing touches to their work makes me smile. It's like rubbing a bit of their love into it, and it all takes time to do it well.

The form

By form, I mean the overall shape and proportions of the elements in a piece. There are a number of good books which provide a great range of profiles for bowls, vessels, boxes and so on (Richard Raffan, *Turning Boxes*; Richard Raffan, *Turning Bowls*; John Hunnex, *Woodturning: A Source Book of Shapes*), so there is no need to repeat those details here.

Suffice to say that the shape of a piece needs to be easy on the eye; that is, to allow the eye to travel over it without any jarring hiccups or inconsistencies. The curves need to be curvy with no bumps or flats. Such curves are generally more pleasing if the angle of curvature is continually varying rather than one that is an exact arc. Variations of width in a whole piece tend to be more attractive than something that is just straight up and down. Changes of direction or edges must be crisp and definite. If a piece is constructed in a number of parts (such as a bowl on a pedestal), the parts must either flow together, or a distinct division should be obvious. As a general rule also, the widest point, or area of greatest detail and interest should be approximately one-third up from the bottom or down from the top. Rules in this game can be broken at times, though!

The proportions of connected elements in a turning will also determine whether a piece is pleasing to the eye. Most turnings are made up of a number of elements. For example, a bowl, box or vessel may have a rim or neck, a body and a foot. There may also be lids, finials, handles, legs, carving, painted design and other attached or protruding parts.

The relationship between these elements, size-wise and structurally is important, as we don't want an otherwise well-executed piece to look top or bottom heavy. The golden section (1:1.618), evident in Fibonacci numbers, in the arrangement of leaves around the stem of a palm tree, in flowers, pine cones, pineapples, spider webs, and used by the Ancient Greeks in their architecture, is a useful guide when considering the comparative sizes of two or more elements within a constructed turning, such as an urn with foot, body and neck.

The design

This is last, but certainly not least. You can have a table full of excellent pieces of turning made from quality, well-chosen wood, well finished and with well-executed shape and proportions. However, as your eye travels over the pieces, there may be one or two that seem to stand out as having something extra. They seem to be more alive, interesting and special. Some judges call it the 'wow' factor. This is where the design of a piece comes in.

In creative terms, design can be defined as having an idea or concept, which is then presented in visual or symbolic form. We see design all around us – in nature, science, in advertisements, company logos, packaging, architecture, art, sculpture and so on. Once you are aware of the existence of design in the everyday things, your mind becomes opened to analysing the ideas behind the visual or material piece. Try studying aircraft logos, cereal packaging or billboards to analyse the message behind the symbols or pictures. Ask yourself, 'What images or ideas in my mind are these pictures or symbols portraying?'; 'what do I think of when I see this logo or ad?'

To translate this idea into the realms of woodturning, let's look at a few specific examples. In the Brisbane International Airport departure lounge is a large, sculptural installation called Anchorage and Passage. It is made from recycled spotted gum and bronze and has a number of different elements making up the whole. To see and appreciate all its elements, you have to view it from a number of angles and from far away and close up. The detail, made up of simple carving, inlays and texturing, on the vertical and cross pieces is most interesting.

The viewer is led to follow the meanders of carved steps and inlaid and textured paths to find little stylized animals and brass plates that you feel compelled to run your fingers over and look in the holes. These details hold a sense of direction (if only a meandering one) and mystery as you move to find out what is around the next corner.

These senses of direction and mystery can also be put into our turnings. We can achieve a sense of direction with the shapes we choose, and by the use of carved, cut, painted or routed curves that sweep upwards or around, or seem to lead the eye from the outside to the inside or vice versa. We put mystery into our work when the viewer can't take it all in, in the one viewing or from the one angle. The work has to be turned around, touched, possibly pulled apart and closely inspected for the whole piece to be understood. It may be that small, hidden details – a little bead bordering the foot of a bowl, a piece of inlay or precious stone on the inside of the lid, a hidden box compartment or a carving in an unexpected place – give that sense of mystery.

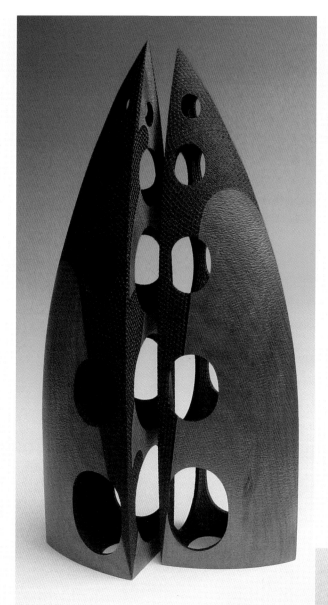

◀ Large multi-centred turning in kauri pine, which also features texturing and pyrography. The external shape of the piece leads the eye up. To understand the detail, the viewer must take it in from a number of angles.

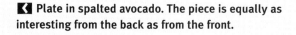
▶ The sandblasting on this piece adds further interest.

◀ Plate in spalted avocado. The piece is equally as interesting from the back as from the front.

128

Freeform carving on the outside of a vessel requires the viewer to look all around the piece to see what is happening on the other side. In a vessel, turning through only a small opening or hollowing from underneath, plugging the opening, then cutting a slit in the side of the vessel, adds that bit of mystery and encourages the viewer to look or try and poke a finger in to see what's inside.

A unity in all elements of form also needs to be evident in our designs. So, if a piece of turning which is highly textured and coloured is placed on a stand, there needs to be a link in the style (in other words, the texturing, the colouring, the line, or all three) of both the piece and the stand.

The little details in the not-so-obvious places require the viewer to explore the piece thoroughly to take it all in and understand it.

◀ These little fragrance flasks are designed to hold drops of fragrant oils. The oil gradually soaks into the wood and a delicate fragrance permeates the room in which they are kept. They are one of my most popular production items. It is the stoppers (which take longer to make than the bases) that give the flasks their appeal. Take away the stopper and you have a fairly ordinary shaped little vase. Note that the decorated or detailed part of the stoppers mirrors the shapes of their respective bases, thus giving a sense of unity to the whole.

The same shape in the finial and legs gives this fluid little box its unity.

Turned, carved and burnt little bowls. What were the maker's sources of inspiration?

New designs for pieces don't often automatically happen. They are usually the result of a long process of development and the building up of a mental bank of ideas. Some turners maintain a sketchbook, no matter how crude, of these ideas. The stimulus for them can be anywhere. Most turners gain stimulus from others – looking at their work, reading books, browsing websites and going to demonstrations. However, there are many other sources of stimulation. Try books on pottery and sculpture; look at nature – landscapes, plants, animals, weather maps, patterns in road cuttings, geological and tectonic movements; look into human history and explore primitive art forms, Greek pottery, baroque art and architectural styles, art deco and art nouveau styles and minimalist modern and postmodern styles. Develop cultural themes; look at human nature – our hopes, dreams, our perversity, our need for recognition, security, excitement, our greatness and baseness; explore spiritual themes – worship of a greater being, fall and redemption. Any of these areas may provide ideas that we can translate, in symbolic form, into our work.

132

In his website, Fred Wiman, a turner from Florida, writes about his mind having 'a Room of Creative Design', occupied by creative gnomes of various predilections.

'At the centre of the room is a table with a large drawing pad. The gnomes, when you can actually get them to sit down and work, will reason and argue and scribble until they have put together "The Picture".

'I have at least four prominent gnomes and a host of minor, sometimes annoying, gnomelets. One gnome, "Bubba", is a traditional, blue collar gnome who directs the shapes of most of my vessels. The shapes, like the gnome, are really quite simple. "Buddha", another gnome, adds an oriental touch to many of my designs. The third prominent gnome, "Bud", is somewhat of a biologist who is taken with the structural pattern of flowers and the microscopic anatomy of plankton. And the fourth gnome is more of a demon who draws from my inner conflicts to add a bit of an edge to some of my designs. "Bud" teams up with the demon to produce lots of pointy things – thorns, teeth, and so on.

'And you thought it would be difficult to explain where designs come from. Pity the gnomeless.

'But remember two things: first, you must encourage and pamper your gnomes. And second, there has never been a gnomeless woodturner.'

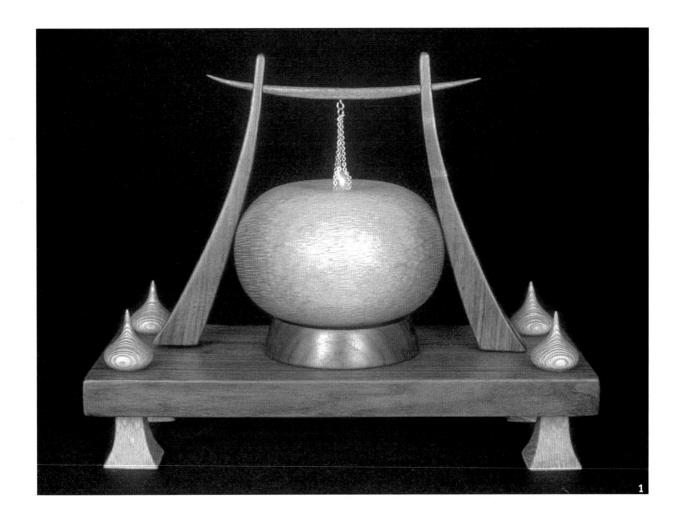

1

'Meditation' **1** ; 'Penthouse for
Nighthawk, with Persian Rug' **2** ; and
'When Jupiter Comes Dancing' **3** .
And Jupiter does dance – it spins on
its base. Can you see the influences of
Fred's creative gnomes in these
pieces?

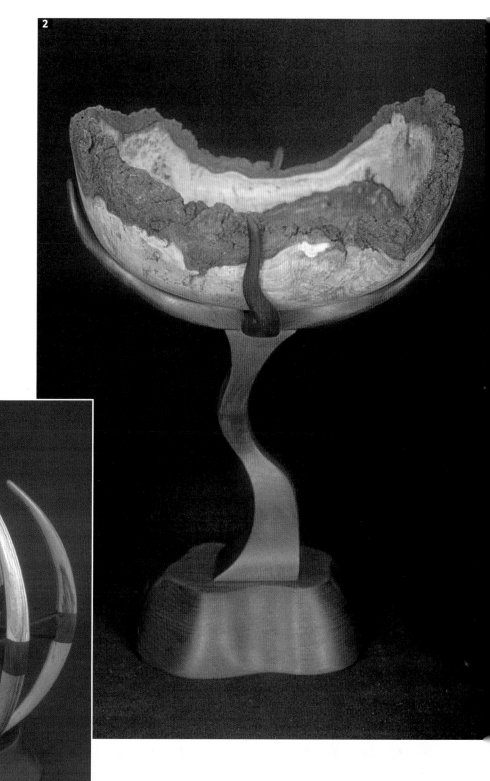

134

All gnomes aside, analyse the pieces by Fred to see where his stimulus came from. Note also, that Fred uses a drawing pad to jot down ideas. Once the ideas start coming, they often come thick and fast and you need to record them before they are forgotten. Get them down, no matter how badly, and you can always refer to them and revise them later. I know of a few turners who keep sketchpads beside the bed at night. They say seriously that it is at night when the ideas start coming. They have to jot the ideas down when they come. If left until the morning, the ideas, like dreams, have passed.

In the last few years, there has also been a movement towards collaboration of turners amongst themselves and with artists working in other media. Large, organized collaborative camps, club or small group collaborations or collaborative partnerships allow for a cross-fertilization of ideas and provide great stimulus for those who take part.

Constructive criticism of each other's work, along with collaboration, can also bring about the development of new ideas and improvement of existing ones. The practice of show-and-tell at some clubs, when done openly, honestly and with some sensitivity, can be very valuable for participants who wish to develop their technical and design capabilities. There's not too many of us who work well in a vacuum.

For those of us who are serious about design, it is important for each turner to develop his or her own style of work. Certainly, while we are working at mastering techniques, imitation of others is necessary. That's what demonstrations and books are for. However, once the techniques are mastered, we need to move on to experiment with and refine our own forms of expression. While that is happening among woodturners, turning will continue to be an exciting and rewarding pastime or profession.

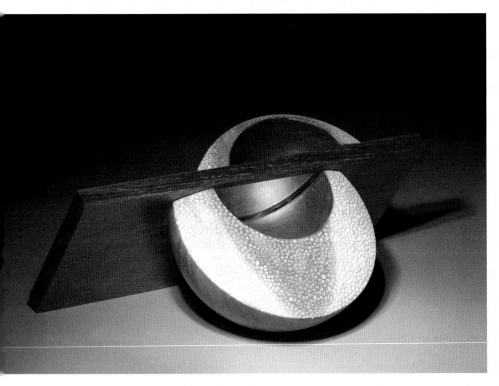

◄ A collaborative piece, which gave us the opportunity to play with off-centre work, cutting and gluing, incorporating mirrors and colouring and texturing. It was a good learning exercise.

► 'Stressed Froggie'. Another collaborative piece made at an organized collaboration in Mittagong, New South Wales.

12

The Decorated Surface

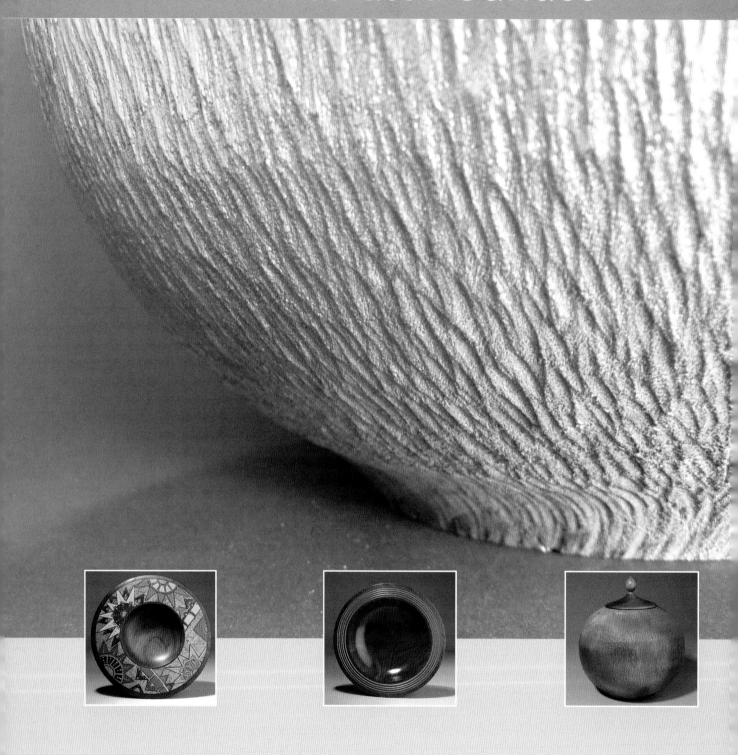

Glues for segmented and laminated work

Wood moves. It expands and contracts according to surrounding temperatures and humidity. At times, it causes us grief when, in dry conditions, a piece that we thought was well seasoned starts to crack, or joints in laminated pieces start to come apart.

To reduce the likelihood of the latter, we need a glue that is first strong and secondly, flexible. It pays to shop around and check out the specifications of the wood glues on the market. A cross-linking PVA glue should give the necessary strength. Yellow aliphatic resin glues are also a popular choice. These are strong, set fast and are relatively elastic. I also know other turners who do a lot of segmented work who swear by the epoxy glues. One that has been recommended to me is Techniglue. The epoxies set fast, soak into end grain and do not lose bonding power when used for gap filling. Nor do they need clamping. However, there is a tendency for them to be brittle. Adding a bit more hardener should increase the elasticity of the cured glue. Epoxy is toxic, so gloves must be worn when working with it.

Whichever glue you choose, many problems can be avoided by making sure that the wood used is very well seasoned, and that segments to be glued together fit well and the surfaces to be joined are free from oil (even from your hands) and dust. Do a dry run first to make sure the fit is good. Clamping should be relatively light – just enough for small beads of glue to squeeze out. Large rubber bands will often serve as clamps.

Routing on the lathe

We can use the router, or its little sister, the trimmer, in conjunction with the lathe indexer, to produce decorative grooves or slits in radial patterns on faceplate work.

On spindle work, such as vases, table legs and so on, we can cut straight or barley twist grooves vertically on the piece and cut recesses in order to insert contrasting timbers. Most of this can be done with the aid of a table arrangement held in the tool post of the tool rest banjo and a trimmer mount, which makes it possible to slide the trimmer across the table with the work held in the lathe. This is a fairly rudimentary form of ornamental turning.

A trimmer set up in a commercial mount on a table, ready for cutting straight grooves in the turned piece.

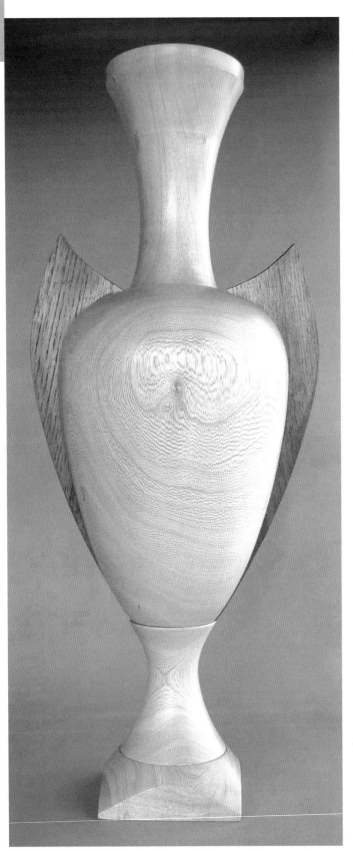

Jacaranda urn with red cedar wings, 30in (762mm) high. Grooves in the body of the urn were cut on the lathe with the trimmer in preparation for inserting the wings.

However, we do not have to be restricted to cutting just straight or barley twist lines on our turnings. Glenn Roberts of New South Wales uses the router in conjunction with a template to produce spirals on his work. The template is temporarily attached, with hot melt glue, to the top of the piece and the router (fitted with a guide bush) is used to cut a spiral effect.

If we try using a template, we don't even have to restrict ourselves to just cutting spirals. If the design requires, we can cut recesses right, or part way, across the work or even deeper segments in already turned grooves. This is an area which has been explored by a few, but not many, turners.

Detail of 'Whorl' showing the central spiral and textured, radiating grooves.

▶ The router, the template and the finished product – a hollow form in coolabah, 11¾in diameter x 3⅛in high (298 x 80mm).

◀ Glenn Roberts with his award-winning coolabah wall sculpture, 'Whorl'. The piece is 30½ x 23½in (770 x 600mm) and has been turned, carved with radial grooves, bleached and the central spiral inserted from behind. The spiral was done with a router on Glenn's converted lathe. He has made similar pieces and routed the radial grooves instead of carving them.

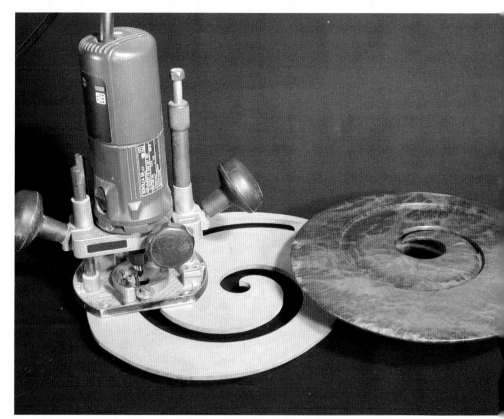

Painting

There are many paints and techniques that can be applied to turned surfaces. We can use enamels, lacquer-based paints, oil paints, water-based acrylics and water-based dyes, inks and paints. The latter – the water-based dyes, inks and some paints – are translucent, allowing the wood grain to show through. They have been discussed in chapter 10, 'Finishing', so will not be covered here. The techniques you can employ to paint a turned surface are varied. The few samples of work shown below illustrate some of those techniques.

The application of colour on these tops is a very simple process. The paint is spray enamel, which is very runny. The top is sanded and a coat of sanding sealer applied and buffed. White paint and at least one other colour are used. A small amount of paint is squirted into the can lid and the can inverted and cleared of paint.

With the top still spinning on the lathe, white paint is applied to the centre of the top with a small brush. Centrifugal force will cause the paint to radiate out in lines. The faster the lathe, the more and thinner the lines. Wipe the white paint off the brush with a rag and repeat the process with the chosen colour or colours. This process can also be used on bowl rims effectively except that it is sprayed directly from the can with the nozzle held very close to the centre of the rim. If desired, spray lacquer or wax can be applied carefully over the enamel, but not oils.

▶ 'Tropical Moon' vase painted in acrylic house paints. The base colour was applied, then the main shapes were painted freehand and the highlights and shadows were applied last of all.

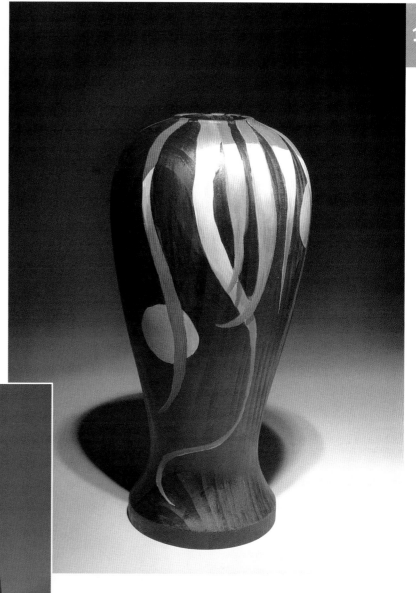

◀ 'Pelicans'. The pelicans were relief carved and coloured with liming solution and food colouring. The black background was obtained using iron filings and vinegar solution.

◀ 'Retro' vase. This was carved on the lathe with an Arbortech mini-carver. Green acrylic paint applied all over and dried; brown paint was applied all over and then wiped off the high points while still wet. It was given a lacquer finish.

▶ Red cedar bowl painted using acrylics. The edges of the rim to be painted are masked off using masking tape that is stretchy and flexible. The base colours (aqua, dark blue and yellow) are sponged on together. When the base is dry, the main shapes are painted on using stencils. Final details, lines and dots are applied freehand.

▶ 'Swords on Blue', an experimental collaborative piece. The brickwork is turned and routed. The size of the bricks had to be calculated for each circle The edges were masked and blue and white spray enamel paint applied in differing concentrations. A stencil of the sword shapes was cut, laid over the piece and black paint sprayed through the cut areas.

144

Green-turned eucalyptus bowls. After the carving out of shapes, a similar process to that on the 'Retro' vase was employed, along with the use of raked texturing paste to give the raised colour.

▶ Burdekin Plum bowl. Grooves were cut in the rim. Successive coats of blue spray enamel were sprayed from one direction onto the grooves with the work spinning slowly, leaving it to dry between coats. Purple spray was then applied from the opposite direction. The overspray was turned and sanded off. The colours change with every movement of the bowl.

◀ Three-sided vessel painted using masking techniques, stencils and hand work.

'Chinese Gold Mine'. Gold leaf applied over a water-based dye. Red acrylic was also brushed lightly over the top of the gold leaf.

Gilding

Gilding involves the application of gold or copper leaf to a turned surface. The leaf is available from most art suppliers and usually comes in packs of a number of sheets. You also need size, which comes in a small can or jar and is applied to the surface to be gilded, and an artist's brush, with which to apply the leaf.

Gold leaf, especially, is wafer thin and cannot be handled with bare hands. If you try, it will stick to your hands, tear and disintegrate. Also, make sure you are applying the gold leaf in a room where the air is still. A slight breeze will blow the leaf everywhere.

The gold size is applied to the surface and left to become tacky. A soft artist's brush is then rubbed in the hair to pick up static electricity.

Use the brush to pick up small pieces of leaf and transfer it to the tacky sized surface. Aim to be accurate in where you place it, because once it touches the surface, it can't be moved. Pat it down gently with the brush. If there is some overlap of the leaf and some of it doesn't stick, this can be brushed away later.

Gold leaf looks good if it is applied in conjunction with colours. You can put a water-based dye on the wood before applying the leaf and letting some of the colour show through. Alternatively, you can brush or spin some acrylic paint over the leaf once the size is dry and let the gold show through the paint. For small pieces, just a little tends to look better than a lot.

'Australian Countrymen's Platter' in camphor laurel, acrylics, found objects and resin. This was a collaborative piece. The earthy colours were chosen to represent the Australian outback. Found objects – leaves, seeds, coins, gum nuts, shells, fishing hooks, a miner's safety hook and ore – all come from central Queensland. Four successive layers of resin were poured to cover these objects.

Resins

Resins are a good and relatively simple way of filling voids or including a decorative rim on a bowl or vessel. You can get casting resin and hardener from some woodturning suppliers or from industrial and hobby fibreglass suppliers. Occasionally, you can also get it from paint suppliers. This can be applied clear or mixed with commercial colours or powder paints to get the colours you want. You can also use metal powders to get a metallic look – gold, copper, silver or bronze. Mix the colour or metal powder with the required amount of resin, add the drops of hardener, pour into the void or recess and allow it to set before turning back and finishing. There are a few important things to beware of when using resin:

■ It is toxic. Wear disposable rubber gloves and a good gas mask.

■ When the hardener is added to the resin, a chemical reaction occurs, the temperature increases and the resin expands. As it cools, it contracts and the resin pulls away from the sides of the hole you thought you filled. Higher temperatures are the enemy. To keep temperatures down, slow down the reaction by adding less hardener than the instructions on the can or, if you are filling a large void, only mix a small amount of resin and hardener and do a number of successive shallow pours to fill the hole. Once you see the first pour start to gel (1–3 hours), mix and pour the second one.

■ Leave the resin a few days to cure before turning and sanding. Turn gently to avoid chipping and cracking. Sand lightly to 2,500 grit wet-and-dry sandpaper, then use car cutting compound or toothpaste for the final polishing.

148

When the hardener is added to the resin, a chemical reaction occurs, the temperature increases and the resin expands. As it cools, it contracts and the resin pulls away from the sides of the hole you thought you filled. Higher temperatures are the enemy. To keep temperatures down, slow down the reaction by adding less hardener than the instructions on the can or, if you are filling a large void, only mix a small amount of resin and hardener and do a number of successive shallow pours to fill

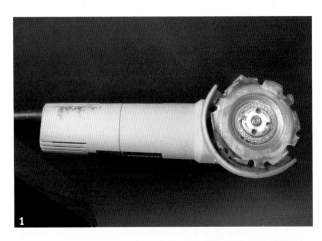

1–**2** Texturing using an Arbortech carver attachment on an angle grinder. Once the piece has been turned to the desired shape, get the tool rest out of the way and spin the lathe slowly. Make sure the piece is secure. Keep your feet wide apart, hold the angle grinder against your body, and use your body to move it across the work. Check the results after a couple of passes.

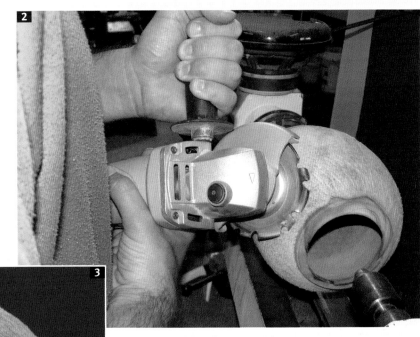

The shape of the indentations created by the grinder will be determined by the angle at which you hold it in relation to the wood. **3**–**5** show the nature of the texturing you can expect. The piece shown in **4** and **5** has subsequently been sprayed with enamel paints.

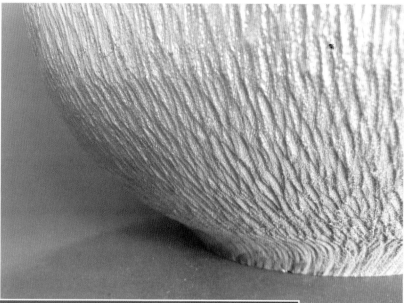

4

5

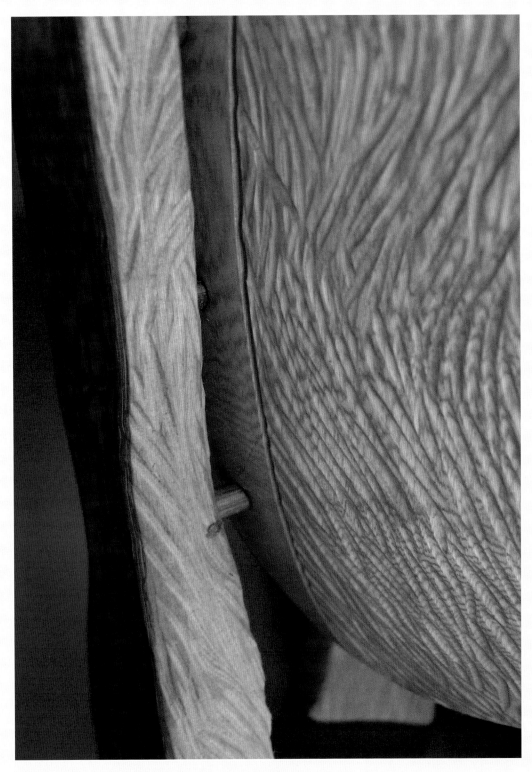

'Lief Feannor' jacaranda vessel textured using a D11/1
hand-carving gouge (very small). The changing directions
of groups of lines can result in some interesting patterns.

'Lotsa Dots' walnut platter, 16½in (419mm) diameter. The textured areas were bleached, then the bleach was carved through with a rotary carving tool to reveal the dark wood in the dots.

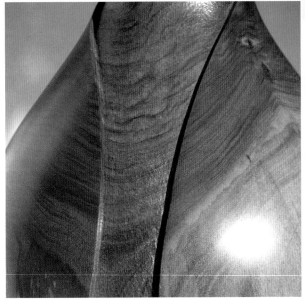

'Penguin Series' in walnut. The detail shows similar orange peel effect to that in the wall shield (see opposite), only this time the maker has used a security engraver with a blunt tip to get a finer texture.

Large kauri pine wall shield, turned and textured with an
air hammer. The result is an orange peel effect. There are
also inserts of slumped glass and stones.

154

Burning

Burning of a finished surface, using a gas flame, then judicious rubbing back with a toothbrush or wire brush can often give a rustic or ancient look to a piece. You can get interesting effects if the burning is also combined with other techniques – colouring, carving or pyrography. Be aware, though, that the heat applied will result in rapid loss of moisture from the wood and some cracking is likely to occur. This may or may not be acceptable, depending on the desired effect.

▶ 'Scorched Castle', a collaborative piece. The vase was first dyed with red water-based dyes, routed, then the outside scorched and rubbed back to reveal some of the red still underneath.

◀ Texture applied with a pyrography pen and hand carving. The sphere was turned, then carved and placed on a tall, carved pedestal.

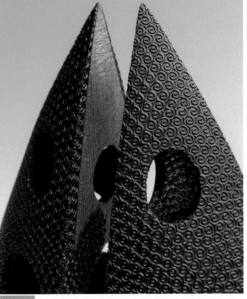

'Reflection'. Texturing was done using
a pyrography pen with the wire in the
shape of a 'koru', the Maori symbol
for new growth, drawn from an
unfolding fern frond.

'Aztec Bird Bath'. This piece was turned in two pieces, carved using the Arbortech mini-carver, burnt with the gas torch, coloured using water-based dyes and inlaid with turned bone. The burnt area was brushed with a toothbrush and re-touched. During burning, keep the gas torch at an angle to the work. If you hold it face-on, the flame will be starved of oxygen and go out.

13

Beyond the Circle

Natural edges

Natural edge work can produce quite spectacular pieces, particularly in timbers that have a marked colour difference between the bark, the sapwood and the heartwood, or where the edge mirrors the grain pattern. This is often the case with natural edge burl bowls.

Whether it be natural edges on spindle or chuck work (vases, boxes, mushrooms and candle holders), or on faceplate work and the production of bowls, the process that you go through is generally the same as you would for an item without natural edges. However, because you are dealing with a rim or an edge that is uneven, you do need to take a few extra precautions.

The first consideration is your choice of wood. Colour is important, but so is balance of the high points, particularly when turning a natural edge bowl. A piece from the trunk of a tree will usually be naturally balanced, with two high points and two low points. If the trunk is not perfectly round or if you intend turning a crotch piece that might have three high pieces where a branch leaves the main trunk, care needs to be taken when deciding where to cut the blank from the log.

The second consideration to be aware of when doing natural edges is lathe speed. If the piece is a bit unbalanced, you may need to run the lathe slower than you normally would. However, you will also need to make clean cuts, especially where natural and turned surfaces meet. A slightly faster speed makes this easier.

'Siblings'. Natural edge nesting bowls in maple burl. The shape of the rims mirrors the curly grain pattern.

Cherry burl natural edge bowl.

It's really a balancing act: having a variable speed lathe helps as you can wind up the speed until vibration starts to occur and then back it off. The point just before the vibration is the optimum turning point for your particular piece.

The third consideration is the bark on the edge. Assuming that you want to keep the bark, it is important to choose a piece of timber that has the reputation for keeping its bark when dry. Inspect the edges a few times throughout the turning process and if there is any sign of bark lifting, glue it back down using superglue (cyanoacrylate) and accelerator. Turn the rim area of a bowl, and get clean cuts before you hollow out the rest of the bowl.

The final, and most important consideration is safety, particularly of your fingers, and especially when finishing the work. Because the rim of a spinning bowl or the outer edges of a natural edge vase are uneven, they will only appear as a shadow. It is very easy to get hand or fingers in the way of the spinning outer edges and it hurts when it happens. On a bowl, you can stick a bit of tape to high points on the rim and leave a short end flapping. That way, if your hand comes near the dangerous bits as you are working the rest of the piece, the flapping tape will give you a warning to move back. Once you reach sanding stage, do not attempt to sand the area near the rim by hand. Power sanding with a large-headed power sander attachment on a drill is the order of the day. Even using the power sander, you have to be careful to angle it so that only the bottom third connects with the wood. If you angle it the wrong way, you are likely to have the end of your attachment knocked off. It also helps to hold the drill against your body so that it is well supported.

160

When sanding spindle work that has natural edges, make sure the tool rest is well out of the way, use long pieces of sandpaper and hold it at both ends with the centre of the paper against the wood. Keep you hands well away.

▶▶ Camphor laurel root bowl, with rounded base and a stand carved out of similarly 'flawed' timber. As the turning progressed, quantities of dirt and stones had to be dislodged from between the roots and regular safety checks made. The rot and cracks in the stand were stabilized with copious quantities of superglue.

Red gum burl bowl. Parts of this bowl also needed stabilizing with superglue, wood dust and resin.

Off-centre bowl

One of the signature pieces of experienced turner John Thompson, of Queensland, Australia, is a small off-centre bowl. This is how he does it.

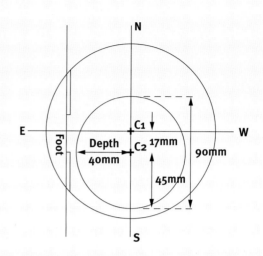

▶ John designs each piece on paper before he starts to get his measurements right. Two lines are drawn at right angles (NS, EW), and a circle which is the outside diameter of the finished piece and centred (C1) at the intersection of the two lines. A third line is drawn parallel to the NS line. The distance between the two is the same depth as the blank to be used. John scribes a second smaller circle with its centre (C2) down the NS line and measures the radius of this circle and the distance between C1 and C2.

The prepared blank is held in using the friction chuck method between the open chuck and the tailstock. The side nearest the tailstock will be the base.

A spigot is turned down. A home-made wooden jig in the shape of a spanner is used to get the right size for the spigot. This will later become the bowl foot.

The outside of the bowl is shaped.

The work is reversed and the spigot is gripped in the chuck. The top of the bowl is faced off and slightly domed.

The centre is marked with a diamond-shaped tool.

The tool rest is brought up to centre height and a line drawn along the face of the bowl.

This line is brought around the underside of the bowl on one side as well.

With this little bowl, John has checked the grain direction with it off the lathe and decided that the bowl recess needs to be offset so that there is cross grain at the thin edge of the rim (where his finger is pointing).

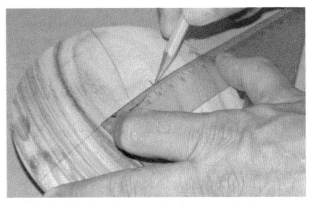

A second line was drawn to reflect the offset position of the bowl recess more accurately. The distance measured on the plan between C1 (the centre of the outside rim – marked while the piece was on the lathe) and C2 (the centre of the offset inside rim) was then marked along the line on the bowl.

This new centre is used to scribe a circle showing where the inside rim will be.

This bowl is an example of something that went wrong. It is very easy to go through the side if the inside rim is too close to the edge, or if the hollowing is too wide down from the rim.

A large disc of fibreboard screwed to a faceplate is mounted on the lathe. There are eleven numbered holes evenly spaced around the edge on one side. These are to hold nuts and bolts to balance the piece when it is mounted off centre.

Two more discs of fibreboard are screwed to the large disc. In the top one, a recess has been turned to take the underside of the little bowl. NS and EW diagonals are marked on the discs. The NS line goes through hole number 6 at the top.

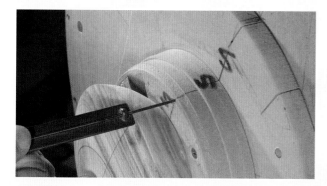

The bowl is placed in the top disc, held in place with the tailstock and is rotated while the level around the rim is checked, using the end of vernier callipers, and adjusted.

The bowl is glued into place with hot melt glue.

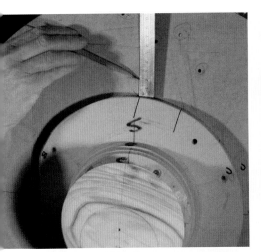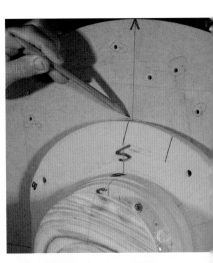

The distance between C1 and C2 is measured south (away from the holes) on the NS line and marked. The top two blocks and bowl are unscrewed and moved along the NS line so the widest edge touches the new off-centre mark. Nails are first driven part way to hold the block steady, and then the block is screwed into this new location and the nails are removed.

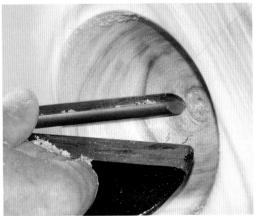

The desired depth of the bowl recess is measured and a depth hole drilled. The bowl recess is turned out with the thickness being checked regularly. Final cuts are done with the round nose scraper.

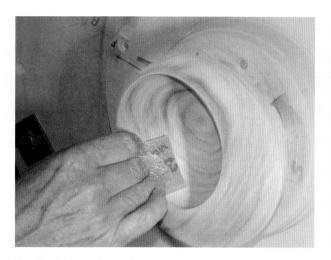

The bowl recess is sanded and sealer applied.

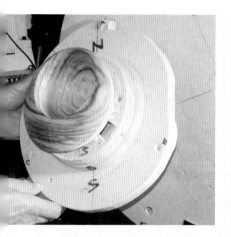

The bowl and supporting discs are unscrewed from the large disc; the two supporting discs are unscrewed and placed, with a cup of water, in the microwave for one minute. This reheats the hot melt glue and the bowl and waste block can be pulled apart.

To remove the bowl from its supporting disc, the two can either be placed in the freezer for a few hours or, if a quicker fix is desired, in the microwave for 30 seconds.

Once warm, the bowl can be prised off the disc. Note the groove in the supporting disc for this purpose; also, the strip of leather between chisel and bowl to prevent damage. Any excess glue on the bowl can be cleaned up.

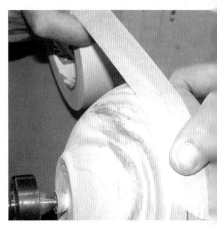

In order to clean up the base of the bowl, a waste block is turned. The bowl is reversed and hot melt glued or taped to the block. The hole in the block doesn't serve any purpose, but just happened to be in the waste block that John had on hand.

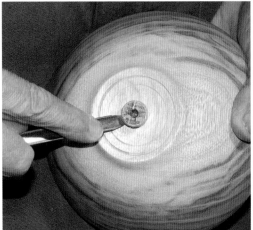

The tailstock is brought up for extra support. The outside and base are cleaned up, both on and off the lathe.

◄ Once finished, John signs the base of each piece of work with a fine point pen.

The finished bowl.

◄ Another one of John's little bowls with stand and finished with high gloss car lacquer recess.

Carved and cut shapes

When we start carving and cutting into turned pieces, there is a good chance that we are moving out of the realms of functionality and into more rarified, decorative, 'artistic' or sculptural pieces. In many ways, it is an attempt to break out beyond the limitations and the 'roundness' of everything that comes off the lathe. A friend who has been turning for many, many years, recently expressed frustration with his turning thus: "I go to the lathe and try to do something a bit different. But in the end, what do I make? Another bowl!" He wanted to move on.

It appears that carving and cutting is the direction that many professional turners and demonstrators are taking in order to move on. The forms that this takes are many and varied and can range from simple decoration of the turned surface with a few gouge marks of the carving chisel to extensive cutting and reassembly of a piece so that evidence of the

'Forest Eyes'. The piece was finished on the lathe but the holding spigot was left on. Surface texturing was applied using two hand-carving gouges. At times, it was done while the work was supported on the lathe; at other times, the piece was on a bean-filled cushion on my lap at the kitchen table. It was time consuming, but hand carving is peaceful and satisfying in the end. The handle on top was turned as an integral part of the lid and then unwanted pieces cut and carved away using the band saw and the Arbortech mini-carver.

Small eucalyptus bowls. Any flaws in the wood are carved or cut out and decoration applied.

initial turning is very difficult to find. So saying, what I cover in this section will only scratch the surface of this topic. The samples shown reflect a few of the many techniques employed.

There is a great range of tools and techniques that can be employed to perform the cutting and carving operations. They vary from the use of the band saw or table saw, small hand saws, hand-carving chisels to angle and die grinders, power carvers (large and small, reciprocal and rotary), drills, power sanding attachments, sanding drums and discs – in fact, anything that cuts or carves wood.

Most turners who have gone down the 'cutting and carving' path and established their own unique style have usually done so by experimenting; 'seeing what happens if I try this'. So, try new things. At worst, you will have another fancy bit of firewood; at best, you will have a masterpiece on your hands.

Standing plate in camphor laurel. Cut on the bandsaw, reassembled and painted.

Turned and cut work: this kauri pine piece was originally turned as a vase but had serious flaws in it. The flaws were simply cut out to make this into an interesting sculptural piece.

170

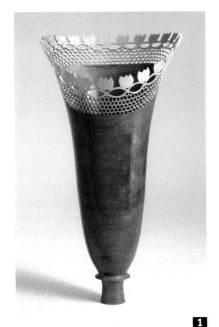

1 **2**

Very fine pierced work in pink ivory by Malcolm Zander. **1** 'Tulipa Rosa'; **2** 'Jellyfish Dressed to Kill'; **3** 'True Love'; and **4** 'Lacemouse'. Malcolm uses quality, dense timbers, turns them very fine and finishes them on the lathe before starting the piercing. Basic outlines for the piercing are pencilled in. Malcolm works with a dental drill and then lightly files off any roughness left by the cutter. Acrylic paints are also applied to some parts.

Malcolm explains the turning of 'Lacemouse': a cylinder is turned between centres, with a tenon at each end, and the mouse profile turned. The piece is cut in half and the front and rear halves separately hollowed out. They are rejoined with a butt joint and superglue. A horizontal line is drawn around the piece, the top half is pierced, and the bottom portion of the mouse then cut away. The tail is turned between centres, boiled, clamped in a mould to set, and attached to the body with superglue.

3

4

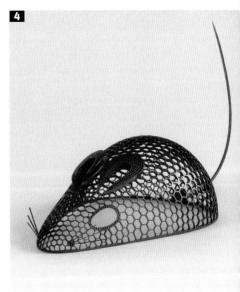

Turned, cut and carved work. **1** Blue gum, New Zealand hibiscus and brass rods with burnt stand; **2** coolibah, acrylics and turned resin base. The maker obtains his resin for turning as leftovers from local surfboard manufacturers.

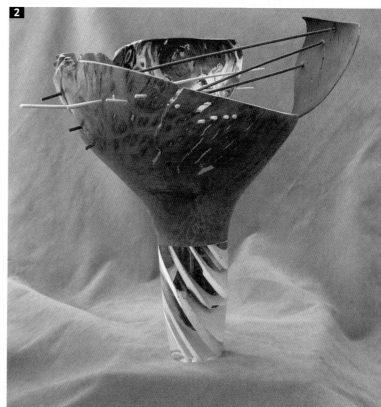

14

Deep Hollowing

Basic principles

Deep hollowing on the lathe is potentially very dangerous. You don't enter the realms of the deep hollow ill equipped. The good news though is that the human mind enjoys a challenge and in recent years, the minds of experienced turners and toolmakers have been turned to meet the challenge of the dangerous deep hollow. We now have on the market an array of chuck jaws, steady rests, jigs and heavy duty, long tools to make deep hollowing more accessible for the average turner.

■ When hollowing, the tip of the tool is often a long way from the tool rest. The further the tool tip is away, the greater the leverage and the greater the chance of a dangerous catch. The turner needs tools that are long and solid enough to withstand the pressures exerted by this great leverage.

■ When working through small openings, the turner can't see the end of the tool and must rely on feel and measurement.

■ Waste material builds up inside the hollow and the lathe must be stopped frequently and the waste cleared either by hand, by blowing through a plastic tube, or with a vacuum cleaner or compressor.

■ The piece being worked is long and often heavy and is usually not being supported by the tailstock when hollowing starts. It needs to be mounted very securely on the lathe.

■ The lathe and its stand must be solid enough to swing large pieces and prevent vibration.

■ Deep hollowing involves cutting into end grain. A hole the depth of the hollowing must first be drilled and then the hollowing tools are used to open up that hole. Work proceeds from the tailstock end down towards the headstock, ensuring that the area being worked is being supported by material closer to the headstock.

Jacaranda and red cedar urn, 34in (863mm) high. Main body and foot were turned separately.

The tools

To hold the work on the lathe, the turner can either use a solid faceplate with many large screws, or a large chuck.

If using a faceplate, the piece must be first roughed down to a cylinder and the ends faced off so that the stock will sit flat on the faceplate. Screws hold better in cross grain than end grain, so the more screws used and the longer they are the better. If the wood is very soft you can drill a series of holes into the sides of the stock near the faceplate and glue dowels into these holes. Once the glue is dry, you can then screw the stock to the faceplate, making sure that the screws go into the dowels. That way, they are holding onto cross-grain timber and will be a lot more secure.

Alternately, a large chuck (I use a Vicmarc 140) with either long shark jaws or wide dovetail jaws can be used. Once the piece is mounted, lock the chuck off securely.

In the last few years, various deep hollowing tools by different manufacturers have appeared on the market. The cutting end of most of them consists of either a ring or hook or a small bar or round scraper. Some of the ring cutters have adjustable limiters to control the amount of cut the tool makes, thus reducing the possibility of catches. These cutters are mounted on either straight or curved (some adjustable) shafts. The important feature about the shafts is that they need to be solid. Finally, a lot of the tools have detachable handles to make the tool easier to store. To take the tools one step further, some come with specially constructed tables, guides or tool supports which either work in conjunction with or replace the tool rest. Hollowing tools are more expensive than standard turning tools. If you are thinking of buying some, it would pay to research the makes of tools available in your locality (or by mail). Read up on them, watch them being demonstrated or, better still, try them yourself before making the final decision.

Besides the cutting tools, the turner will utilize a solid Jacob's chuck and long drills (saw tooth bits, auger bits or large twist drills on an extension bar) and callipers to measure wall thickness. A few deep hollowing sets have an inbuilt laser light system to indicate wall thickness as the turner is hollowing.

The large Vicmarc VM140 chuck with shark jaws and wide dovetail jaws.

1–**2** The Munro hollowing tool. The handle is made of hollow, light aluminium. The tool shaft slides into the handle and is locked in to the desired length. The ring cutters have adjustable limiters over them to control the depth of cut, and an extra articulated head (see **1**) for undercutting can be fitted.

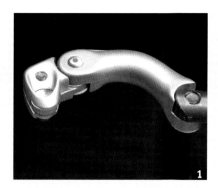

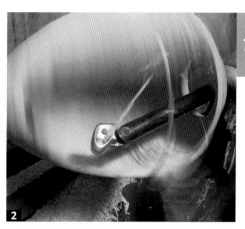

◄ The Vermec hollowing tool set. From top to bottom: small ring cutter; ring cutter with side limiter; round shear scraper; adjustable side cutter (this operates flat side down on the tool rest); extension shaft and handle. Each shaft fits into the handle and is secured on the machined flat with a grub screw.

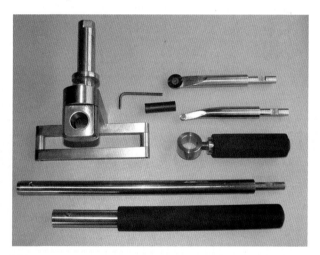

▲ The Vermec Ultimate Hollowing set with tool support, allen key, shear scraper, angled ring cutter and protective sleeve, side handle, extension shaft and main handle.

▲ One of my most used and cheapest hollowing tools, a square section high-speed steel purchased without a handle and either machined to fit into the Vermec handle, or a long, solid, turned wooden handle.

▶ The Vermec Ultimate Hollowing set in action. The gate and pivoting front bush of the tool support hold the tool steady as it cuts the back of the piece, on the upswing. The operator is able to swing the tool sideways and backwards and forwards. The ring cutter is used for waste removal and is then replaced by the shear scraper for finishing cuts. The tool support held in the tool post takes away a lot of the jolting experienced with hand-held hollowing tools.

Methods

To turn a large vase or urn, first mount the stock between centres and rough-turn the outside shape. Either turn a spigot to fit into chuck jaws or face off the end if you are going to mount it on a faceplate. Transfer the work to the chuck or faceplate and mount it on the lathe. Using a long auger bit, ½–1in (13–25mm), or a large saw tooth bit, drill a central hole the length that you want hollowed.

Start the hollowing by opening out the neck as wide as you want it, working from the centre out. Then, work at opening up the shoulder area, undercutting if necessary, and gradually work down deeper until the required depth is obtained. You won't be able to see what is happening, so most of the work will have to be done by feel.

You will have to stop the lathe often to clear out the shavings. This can be done relatively easily using either the air compressor or a vacuum cleaner. This will also give you a chance to check wall thickness and depth.

When using long-handled tools, I find it easier to work from the back of the lathe and tuck the handle of the tool under my arm. That way, I don't have to lean over the lathe bed and my whole shoulder helps control and absorbs any jarring that comes from the tool tip hitting uneven wood. This is easier for a short person, and for a left-hander more so than for a right-hander.

Sanding the inside of the vase or urn may be difficult, depending on the width of the opening. You could use sandpaper glued to a round stick. Alternatively, tool the best finish possible, give sanding a miss and then blacken the inside with matt black spray paint.

Finish refining the outside shape, then sand and apply your finish and part the piece off.

Drilling a central hole with a large saw tooth bit before opening it out with the hollowing tools. These large bits are very stable, but don't normally handle cutting end grain well, so the wood must be green or naturally soft.

Tucking the tool handle under my armpit and working from the back of the lathe.

With large pieces, it is a good idea to part down until the piece is being held by about ½in (13mm) of wood. Then, the lathe can be turned off and the last piece sawn through with a hand saw. Sand the base using a power sanding attachment and apply the finish to the base.

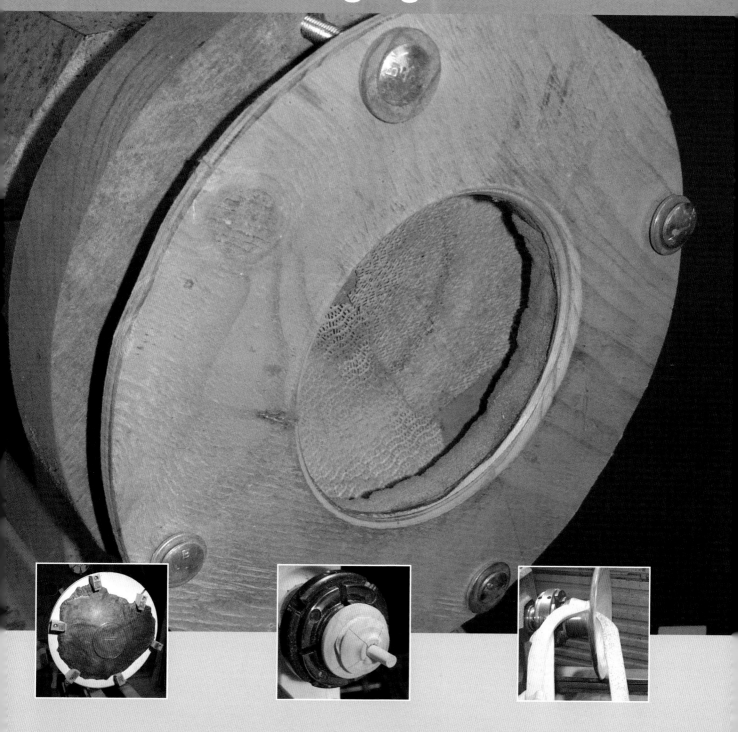

15

Using Jigs

Jigs to help you hold work on the lathe, to help you cut accurately or to measure accurately can be very simple or very complicated. Here are a few, starting with the most simple.

1 Wooden scrap ends from spigots and spindle work are handy because they already have centres marked in them. Flatter ones can be held on the tailstock point and pressed up against work, which you don't want to be marked by the tailstock point. Wider ones can be used if you have hollowed a vase and wish to bring the tailstock up for support while you do the finishing cuts to the outside. Save the good ones and keep them in a large plastic jar. More scrap blocks are shown in **2**. Amongst other things, larger blocks can be used to make jam-fit chucks for holding small boxes when you need to tidy up the base.

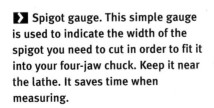 Spigot gauge. This simple gauge is used to indicate the width of the spigot you need to cut in order to fit it into your four-jaw chuck. Keep it near the lathe. It saves time when measuring.

1–**4** Bowl reversing chuck for finishing off the base of a bowl. You can buy plates and jaws that screw onto your chuck to do this, but they aren't cheap and changing the jaws over is time consuming, so there's no reason why you can't make one. John Hanrahan made this one. A large disc of fibreboard or plywood (this one is coated with melamine) is glued and screwed to a smaller disc which can either have a recess for gripping in the chuck, expansion mode; or it can be screwed to a faceplate ring or old video player head to be gripped, contraction mode, in the chuck. Alternatively, the disc could be attached to a dedicated faceplate made from a flat piece of steel welded to a nut with the same thread as the lathe spindle.

With the disc in the lathe, use the indexer and rout six slots in the disc. The central circle in the front of the disc indicates the diameter of the back holding disc. John has also drilled a hole near one edge for hanging purposes. The edge of the disc is then taped for protection. Sets of six buttons, angled on the inside and padded with leather or foam are then cut and drilled. These are attached through the slots with a bolt and wing nuts and can be moved in and out to accommodate the size of the bowl being held. A number of sets of buttons can be made, with different heights and angles, to accommodate different shaped bowls. The tailstock is brought up at first for extra safety and later removed for sanding.

Sanding discs and drums in various stages of wear. For the discs, drill a circle in a flat blank. It needs to be large enough for the chuck jaws to fit into it; a saw tooth bit or Forstner bit will do the job. Mount the blank on the lathe, trim it down to a circle and face it off. You can either glue sandpaper directly onto the surface or glue on a disc of Velcro (removable discs of Velcro-backed sandpaper can be obtained). Make a sanding table by turning down a cylinder to fit into the lathe tool post. If you intend using this regularly, the wood will wear. You could sheath the wooden cylinder with a metal tube that fits into the tool post. Drill a hole the same diameter as the cylinder in a dressed rectangular block approximately 10in (254mm) long, 5in (127mm) wide and ¾in (19mm) thick. Glue in the cylinder and fit it into the tool post. The sanding drums are simply sandpaper glued onto different sized cylinders. They come in handy for all sorts of jobs.

⌵ A holding cage can be used for reverse chucking bowls to clean up their bases and to remove the holding spigot on bud vases (below). The supporting base is held on the chuck with a video player head. It is dished in the centre to support the convex shape of the front of the bud vases and has a disc of non-slip cloth glued on with contact cement. Drill four holes to accommodate the bolts and wing nuts that join the base and the top plywood holding plate. Glue a circle of foam to the inside of this plate to prevent damage to the work. Blanks for the vases are held by the friction method against the four-jaw chuck and a spigot is turned. The point marked by the tailstock is important for centring in the cage. Grip the spigot in the chuck. Turn and finish the front of the vase, and as much of the back as possible. Drill the hole to hold the glass tube. With the cage mounted on the chuck, remove one or two bolts, insert the vase, back side out and bring up the tailstock to centre it using the marked point in the spigot. Tighten the top plate down and remove the tailstock in order to turn off the spigot. Slow the lathe speed and make fine cuts. Off the lathe, cut off one side to form the base.

1–**2** Off-centre spindle chuck. This simple chuck, designed by John Thompson to fit in a four-jaw chuck, will enable you to turn small spindle work off-centre. It consists of a disc, screwed to a bar on one side and a block on the other. The block has a wide hole drilled to take a spigot holding the workpiece. Simply grip the bar between two of the jaws; loosen it and slide it along when you want to turn off-centre. The tape in **1** is a warning device, designed to flap if you get your hand too close.

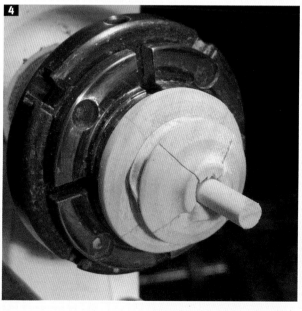

3–**4** This dowel-holding jig is handy if you haven't got a chuck with pin jaws. Drill a hole in a scrap disc just smaller than the dowel you wish to grip. Turn the disc to the shape shown, making sure to turn a cove to hold the rubber band, then cut and number the pieces. Keep the rubber band around the pieces when not in use. Simply loosen the chuck jaws to insert and remove the dowel.

5–**6** Drilling jig. This is made of three small blocks of wood for the base and sides (glued and screwed at 90°), and a wooden lever, held in place with a nut and bolt. To hold the block to be drilled, raise the back of the lever.

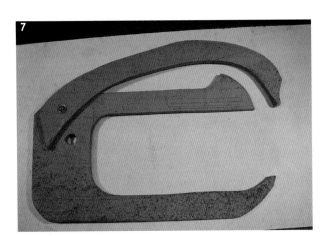

7–**8** Thickness gauge. This consists of one fixed shape of plywood, and one swinging arm. The thickness of the turned wood is indicated where the line on the swinging arm meets the line(s) on the fixed arm.

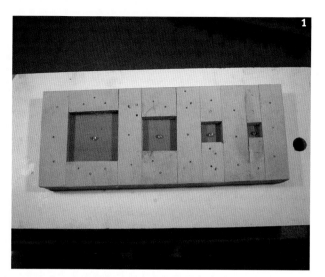

1–**3** Centre-find box. This jig is similar to the one featured in chapter 7, except that you have a number of different sizes from which to choose. Press the square block into the appropriate hole, twist it so the corners meet the edges of the box, then tap sharply with the hammer. The screw in the centre of each of the squares will leave an indentation on the end of the wood.

4–**5** Power sanding attachments. These are made of parts from old video players, rubber sheet and Velcro, glued with heat-resistant contact cement.

Glossary

Bead
Beads are the semicircular convex decorations on turning. They are done mostly, but not always, on spindle turning and are often done as a series of beads or in conjunction with coves and fillets (see **1**).

Between centres
This refers to wood that is being held on the lathe between the headstock and tailstock. Spindle turned work is held 'between centres'.

Bevel
The bevel is the part of the tool that has been ground just behind the sharp edge.

Blank
The wood, usually cut to size, ready for mounting on the lathes (see **2**).

Burls (burrs)
Burls or burrs occur on trees where, at some stage, the tree has been injured. Wood has grown around the injured area. They often appear as rough bulges off the side of the tree trunk. The timber in burls is often highly figured with wild grain going in all directions. Sometimes the wood in burls is very unstable with cracks and bark inclusions. However, because of the interesting grain, burls are highly prized by woodturners.

Cam lock
The arrangement for locking tool rest banjos and tailstocks onto the lathe bed. Cam lock systems are standard on all lathes now and they make locking and unlocking tool rest banjos and tailstocks so easy, compared to the old nut-and-bolt arrangements (see **3**).

Casting resin
Casting resin is an epoxy that comes in two parts – the resin and the hardener. It can be coloured or used clear to fill holes (natural or man-made) in the wood.

Cove
A cove is a semicircular concave decorative recess usually done in spindle work, and often bordered by fillets and beads (see **1**).

Chuck
Chucks are used to hold the wood for turning on the lathe. They usually have four jaws, which can be made to expand or contract to grip the work (see chapter 1).

Cross grain
Think of wood as a series of fibres. The direction in which the fibres lie is the grain. If a piece of wood is mounted on the lathe so that the grain direction is across or at right angles to the lathe bed, you will be hollowing cross grain. This is usually the case when you are doing faceplate or bowl work.

Dead centre
Dead centres are rarely used now, but in the past, they fitted into the tailstock and were used to hold spindle work on the lathe. Unlike the present live tailstock centres they weren't fitted with bearings and didn't spin. To allow the wood to spin on the centre, the turner had to apply grease to the end of the wood. Occasionally, dead centres are now used in the headstock for light spindle work where marks from the drive centre are unwanted.

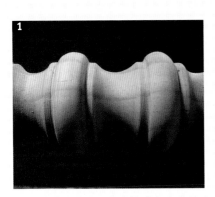

1 Beads, fillets and coves.

2 Blanks cut ready for faceplate turning.

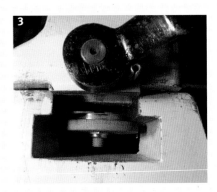

3 Cam lock on a tailstock.

4 Tailstock centres – cup and cone style – and drive centre (left) with spurs to fit in the headstock.

5 Faceplates.

6 End grain being faced off.

Drive centre

The drive centre fits into the headstock and is used for spindle work. It usually has a centre point surrounded by a number of prongs that dig into the wood and force it to spin once the lathe is switched on (see **4**).

End grain

End grain occurs where the log or plank has been cut. It needs to be sealed if the wood is to be stored for drying. End grain can be hollowed, for example, when holding a piece in a four-jaw chuck and turning a goblet or lidded box.

Faceplate

Faceplates come in a number of sizes and are generally used for mounting cross-grain work (mostly bowls) to the lathe. The blank (the wood to be turned) is screwed to the faceplate, which is then in turn screwed onto the headstock (see **5**).

Face off

To face off is simply to tidy up the ends on spindle or end-grain chuck work. It is usually done with a parting tool or skew chisel (see **6**).

Fillet

The fillet is a small, flat shoulder between a bead and a cove (see **1**).

Finials

Finely turned decorative tops on spires, spindle work or lidded boxes.

Forstner bit

Drill bits that feature a small centring point and two planing blades that are surrounded by a sharpened cylinder. They are similar to saw tooth bits. Forstner bits create a very clean cut in cross-grain work, but do not cope well with drilling into end grain unless the wood is green or very soft (see **7**).

Friction chucking

To bring up the tailstock in order to hold a piece of wood on the lathe between the tailstock and the chuck. Friction chucking is usually used for small pieces only. It is often used to start pieces off or for holding a bowl in order to tidy up the base (see **8**).

Headstock

This is the part of the lathe that houses the drive pulleys that make the attached wood spin. The motor may also be housed in the headstock (see **9**).

7 Forstner bit (front) and saw tooth bits (behind).

8 Friction chucking.

9 Lathe headstock.

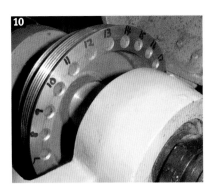

10 Inbuilt indexing system. There are 24 positions in this system.

11 Jacob's chuck and key.

12 Sanding the inside of a bowl using a power sanding attachment mounted in a drill.

Indexing

An indexing system on a lathe enables the user to lock the lathe in place into a number of predetermined, evenly spaced positions, in order to drill or rout decorative grooves. Some lathes have indexing systems built into the pulleys. Indexing systems can also be attached to the outboard (outside end of the headstock) or near or on the chuck (see **10**).

Jacob's chuck

The chuck, named after its inventor, which is used to hold drill bits in the tailstock (or sometimes the headstock) for drilling on the lathe. It can also be used to hold small dowels for turning (see **11**).

Jam chucking

Also known as jam-fit chucking. A method of holding work on the lathe by jamming it into a prepared wooden recess or onto a prepared spigot. It is of particular use when re-chucking a bowl or lidded box to tidy up the base.

Laminating

Gluing strips of wood together.

Live centre

This is the centre that goes in the tailstock and is used to hold spindle work. Live centres are fitted with bearings to enable the point and/or cone of the centre that is in contact with the wood to spin.

Morse taper

The morse taper is the tapered metal part of a drive or tailstock centre that fits into the headstock or tailstock. The number of the morse taper denotes the size of the cylinder on the headstock and tailstock that it fits into. Most lathes are designed to take a number 2 morse taper. Some older lathes and some current mini lathes take a number 1 morse taper which has a smaller diameter (see **4**).

Ornamental turning

The use of indexing, compound slides and a range of specialized cutters to produce highly decorative turnings.

Outboard turning

There are times when the piece you want to turn is too big to fit on the lathe over the lathe bed. Some lathes have the facility to swivel the head of the lathe so that larger pieces can be turned 'outboard', not over the lathe bed.

Power sanding attachment

These attachments can be held in a drill and used to sand work, which is spinning on the lathe. It speeds up sanding large areas considerably. They can also be held in a chuck and be used to sand the bases of end-grain pieces, which have just been parted off (see **12**).

Pulleys

Two sets of stepped discs and a pulley belt connect the motor to the drive shaft in the headstock. Changing the belt on the different sized discs then makes it possible to change the rotation speed on the lathe.

Roughing out

Roughing out is the rough turning of a log, square stock or blank to bring it down to a cylinder before it is shaped.

Segmented turning

Construction of pieces for turning by gluing up numbers of segments or smaller pieces of pre-cut blocks of wood.

Shellac

Shellac is made up of beetles' wings dissolved in denatured alcohol. It is usually used in French polishing or as a sealer.

13 Spalted box elder lidded vessel. The fungus has left the grey, black and orange marks on an otherwise bland piece of timber.

14 A spigot turned on the end of a cylinder.

15 This half-turned piece is made up of staves.

Spalted

When a tree is felled and left in damp weather for a while, fungus may start growing in the wood. This leaves grey, black and sometimes green and orange marks on the wood. Sometimes it is very attractive. Care needs to be taken when turning spalted wood to ensure that you don't breathe in the fungus spores (see **13**).

Spigot

This is a plug turned on the end of a cylinder while being mounted between centres. The spigot, which is dovetailed (angled in towards the shoulder of the cylinder), is then gripped in the chuck jaws for further turning (see **14**).

Spindle turning

Turning of wood that is mounted on the lathe between the drive centre in the headstock and the live tailstock centre.

Stave construction

The gluing together of lengths of wood or staves to form a cylinder in preparation for turning. Old wooden wine barrels were made using stave construction methods (see **15**).

Steady rest

A steady rest is usually used to support long pieces of spindle turning either when the tailstock is not in use (see **10**), or if the turned piece is very long and thin and needs to be supported in the centre to prevent vibration and subsequent breakage. The steady rest in **10** is a solid, commercially-built one. For fine, light spindle work, home-made steady rests can be constructed out of plywood and waxed string.

Stock

The wood that is prepared for mounting on the lathe.

Tailstock

This slides along the lathe bed and helps hold pieces on the lathe (see **16**).

Tool rest

The metal support for the tool as it moves across and cuts the wood.

Tool rest banjo

The arrangement holding the tool rest onto the lathe bed.

Variable speed lathe

A variable speed lathe enables the operator to adjust the lathe speed while the lathe is still running. It can be a mechanical variable speed, which is based on adjusting the width of one of the pulleys, or an electronic variable speed lathe.

16 Tailstock for a deep bed lathe.

About the author

Carol Rix is a professional woodturner from Queensland, Australia. She works mostly in salvaged, recycled local timbers and the hard, dense, colourful desert timbers, and she supplies a number of shops and galleries in the eastern states of Australia. Her work can be seen on her website www.carolrixwoodturner.com

Carol is an experienced teacher and teaches woodturning in her own workshop and demonstrates at clubs and symposiums.

Carol writes regularly for *The Australian Woodworker* and she maintains a website, www.woodturningtips.com on which free, weekly woodturning tips are posted. Visitors to that website can request a tip to answer any question they may have on woodturning.

Woodturning Tips and Techniques: what woodturners want to know is Carol's first woodturning book.

Acknowledgements

As with any venture, we do not work in a vacuum. There are many people who have helped and encouraged me in the writing of this book. Thanks to my son, Graham, who got me started and has managed my websites; to John Thompson who has proofread, photographed and encouraged when the going got tough; to my adopted 'fathers', Eric and Alan, who have been very generous with their help and encouragement; to all those people who have contributed to the book by sending in their questions; finally, to everyone who has allowed me to use photographs of their work. Their ownership and websites have been recognized here.

Makers (where not otherwise credited, turned work is by Carol Rix)

Photographic credits

Carol Rix and the Guild of Master Craftsman Publications gratefully acknowledge the following people for granting permission to reproduce their photographs in this book.

Warren Carpenter 49 (inset, right), 57

John Hanrahan 177 (inset, left), 179 (images 1–4)

Bobby Phillips 186 (image 13), 188

Andrew Potocnik 7 (inset, top), 120 (inset, middle), 127 (bottom), 129 (bottom), 130, 131

Graeme Priddle 127 (top), 155

Glenn Roberts 139

Tom Robinson 5 (inset, left), 8 (inset, left), 54 (top and bottom), 108 (inset, right), 114 (top and bottom), 122 (top), 151, 157 (inset, left), 158, 172 (inset, left and inset, right)

Neil Scobie 144

John Thompson (inset, right), 8 (inset, right), 119 (inset, top), 120 (inset, left), 121, 126, 157 (inset, middle), 167 (middle and bottom), 169 (top)

Lee-Ann Wilson 3, 5 (main image), 7 (inset, bottom), 108 (inset, middle), 112 (bottom), 119 (inset, middle and inset, bottom), 120 (inset, right), 128, 129 (top), 134, 135, 136 (inset, left and inset, middle), 140, 141 (top and bottom), 142 (bottom), 143, 145 (bottom), 147, 154 (top), 157 (main image and inset, right), 160 (top and bottom), 168 (top), 173

Robert Wilson 124, 152, 153

Malcolm Zander 5 (inset, middle), 8 (inset, middle), 159, 170 (all)

Contacts and websites

Ancient Kauri Kingdom www.ancientkauri.co.nz

Caloundra Woodworkers' Club
PO Box 1192, Caloundra 4551. Australia

Carolina Mountains Woodturners
www.carolinamountainwoodturners.org

Tom Goldschmidt www.designedwood.com

Rolly Munro (hollowing tools)
www.rollymunro.co.nz

Northern Rockies Woodworkers' Guild
www.nrwg.org

Graeme Priddle www.graemepriddle.co.nz

Carol Rix www.carolrixwoodturner.com
www.woodturningtips.com

Neil and Liz Scobie www.neilandlizscobie.com

The Australian Woodworker magazine
www.skillspublish.com.au

Karl Tickle Productions
www.ktmp.co.uk

Fred Wiman www.woodturningart.com

Vermec Engineering (hollowing tools)
39 Dalton St, Kippa Ring, Qeenslandd 4021.
Australia

Malcolm Zander www.malcolmzander.com

Index

Guild of Master Craftsman Publications Ltd,
Castle Place, 166 High Street, Lewes, East Sussex BN7 1XU, United Kingdom
Tel: 01273 488005 Fax: 01273 402866 E-mail: pubs@thegmcgroup.com Website: www.gmcbooks.com

Ask us for a complete catalogue, or visit our website. Orders by credit card are accepted.